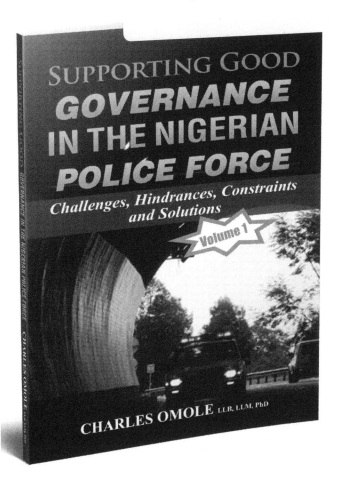

SUPPORTING GOOD
GOVERNANCE
IN THE NIGERIAN
POLICE FORCE

Challenges, Hindrances, Constraints and Solutions

Volume 1

CHARLES OMOLE LLB, LLM, PhD

Supporting Good Governance in the Nigerian Police Force.

SUPPORTING GOOD GOVERNANCE IN THE NIGERIAN POLICE FORCE.

Challenges, Hindrances, Constraints and Solutions.

VOLUME 1

DR CHARLES OMOLE

Supporting Good Governance in the Nigerian Police Force.

ABSTRACT

The Nigerian police like others in post colonial African nations is a creation of the colonial legacy and set up as a tool of repression in the exercise of colonial hegemony over local communities. With military governments in power for most of the nation's independent years, the police institution has been starved of needed resources and operational development opportunities in an effort to remove them as a potential threat to the military maladministration in Nigeria.

Going by the media reports on the social media over the past few years, law enforcement has become a vital tool employed by the state to directly or indirectly violate the rights of its citizen in many African societies. The frontline law enforcement organisation in most countries is the police.

The objective of this study is to assess law enforcement practices in Nigeria and suggest ways of developing and supporting good governance in its operations. This book is not about how Nigerian police can become like those in Western Europe, it is about how Nigerian police can operate within the provisions of the Nigerian constitution and legislative Acts with all its national peculiarities.

Despite a Constitutional mandate that clearly stated that there will be only one federal police force in Nigeria, the governments in power over the past twenty years have created several policing related agencies who exercise policing powers. Some were carved out of the police force, while others created from scratch to investigate and prosecute crimes, which are supposed to be the responsibilities of the police force.

This development has diverted much needed funding away from the police into these various agencies. This has contributed to the major budgetary shortages faced by the police currently.

The foregoing and other factors identified in this book have led to a demotivated, poorly trained, corrupt, badly regarded and ineffective police institution in Nigeria. So the goal of this research is to utilise an unprecedented access given to find out what are the limitations and challenges facing the police in Nigeria. The book also identified ways to support good governance within the Nigerian police in ways that enables the police to deliver on their constitutional mandate.

The research conducted reveals not only how the people see the police, but more profoundly how the police see the police. The access granted to police officers at all levels has allowed for a ground breaking inside view of the world of policing from the perspective of the police. This study found a great deal of correlation between what the public think about the police and what the police think about the police. It makes for a fascinating reading.

This practical research concluded by making over forty recommendations on how good governance can be developed and strengthen within the police. Using both persuasive and dissuasive tools and techniques, these recommendations are wide ranging, balanced and implementable.

The recommendations are then grouped into three categories of those requiring additional funds to implement, those that do not require any new funding (simply a better use of existing funds), and those that actually reduces the money spend on policing.

This book is only volume one of the research into the subject of "supporting good governance in the Nigerian police". It focuses only on the top two groups of challenges (out of five) revealed by the field study. This relates to the funding as well as the recruitment and training of police officers. So there are other areas untouched which would be subject of a future study into this subject.

This book is engaging and profoundly revealing on the challenges facing the Nigerian police, but the recommended actions in the final chapter (when implemented) will promote and strengthen good governance within the police and secure its constitutional legacy as custodian of the civil security of Nigerian citizens and residents.

Lastly, the use of the words "Nigerian Police Force" in the title of this book is deliberate. Officially the police are known as the Nigeria Police Force. That is without an (n) after the word Nigeria. It is my conclusion that there is a desperate need to Nigerialise (so to speak) the police. There is a need to bespoke its operations and rules to reflect the peculiar aspirations and culture of the Nigerian Nation.

Supporting Good Governance in the Nigerian Police Force.

ACKNOWLEDGMENTS

Conducting the research that underpinned this book has been a lot more challenging than I imagined. From the many trips to meetings that never take place in the end, to the virtual scarcity of data and little reference materials to call on.

But this study could not have been completed without the excellent support of many people too numerous to mention by name. My thanks go to Prof. Hatchard, Professor of Law at the University of Buckingham. With his decades of research in several African countries, he was able to nudge my efforts in ways that made the field study more productive.

I will like to thank the Library staff of the universities of Lagos, Ibadan, Ife and Jos (all in Nigeria), that assisted my search for materials, even though I could not find much. My thanks also go to my late uncle, Professor Emeritus T. N. Tamuno who many years ago, deposited the love for the Nigerian Police in my heart through his pioneering work in this field. I can imagine his pride at the continuation of police research work by a member of the family.

Finally, I will like to acknowledge the support of my family who always bear with me and are ever encouraging as I have pursued my many academic endeavours over the years.

One of the possible accusations that can be levelled against this book is that it seems to be too supportive of the police by explaining away their shortcomings. This is not the case.

There are lots of reports already in existence listing the many rot and corruption in the police. From Amnesty International to Human Rights Watch, there are plenty of well documented research and papers on the failures of the Nigerian police.
My goal in this book is to understand the underlying reason why the police act the way they do. I have not sought to explain away their failures; I just feel there is little point in

telling a bad child he is bad. I will rather find out why he is bad and what can be done to clean him up. This has been by aim with this book. I am more interested in how we can support and transform the police than merely castigating them from the outside.

To this end, I will like to thank the dozens of serving and retired police officers that gave me their time. From the low level frontline officers to middle ranking police officers, to the top brasses that cooperated with me and gave me valuable inside information of the challenges facing the police.

As promised to them, I have ensured a complete protection of their confidentiality and anonymity throughout this book.

The virtual non existence of reliable relevant materials and the data void that exist in Nigeria has meant I have had to rely on lots of media reports and interviews given by police officers.

I hope this book will become a reference point

for future researchers on how the Nigerian police can be supported and transformed.

TABLE OF CONTENT

DEDICATION

I will like to dedicate this book to all the genuine and honest Nigerian Police Officers who have died in the course of duty from Independence till date. You may have been few in number but your dedication is appreciated and celebrated.

Supporting Good Governance in the Nigerian Police Force.

ABBREVIATIONS AND ACRONYMS

ACHPR	African Commission on Human and Peoples' Rights
APCOF	African Policing Civilian Oversight Forum
ASSN	African Security Sector Network
AU	African Union
CHRI	Commonwealth Human Rights Initiative
CSO	Civil society organisation
ECOWAS	Economic Community of West African States Association
NIPSA	Network for Improved Policing in South Asia
NGO	Non-governmental organisation

OSIWA	Open Society Initiative for West Africa
RECs	Regional Economic Communities
TOC	Transnational organised crime
UNPKO	United Nations Peace-Keeping Operations
WAPCCO	West African Police Commissioners Cooperation Organisation
WAPORN	West African Police Reform Network
CLEEN	Centre for Law Enforcement Education in Nigeria
NPF	Nigerian Police Force
IMF	International Monetary Fund
IGP	Inspector General of Police

TABLE OF FIGURES

Supporting Good Governance in the Nigerian Police Force.

INTRODUCTION

In the 1980s, the International Monetary Fund (IMF) and World Bank had a policy of Structural Adjustment Programmes designed and imposed as conditionality of lending to many developing countries.[1] The criticism of this one size fits all approach was its lack of adaptability to national peculiarities and esoteric factors. The IMF has since abandoned this bland approach after resistance by many from the developing world.

It can be argued that this applies to global law enforcement, democracy and standard of the

---

[1] 'Structural Adjustment' (Wikipedia, 2016)
<https://en.wikipedia.org/wiki/Structural_adjustment>
accessed 11 January 2016

rule of law operating in nations of the world. Just like capitalism, law enforcement practices will be different from nation to nation. The self adaptive nature of capitalism[2] is a growing area of economic study. This shows that Capitalism is not practiced the same way, even in the Western economies.

For instance, we have the highly deregulated private sector led UK economy, but a highly centralised, public sector led French economy. Yet both are Capitalist nations. This author has concluded there is the same need for national slants to law enforcement operations but stabilised by some universally accepted standards.

So there cannot be a one size fits all approach to law enforcement standards and criminal justice jurisprudence globally given the many peculiarities and primordial contexts that exist

---

[2]John Fullerton, 'Regenerative Capitalism' < http://capitalinstitute.org/wp-content/uploads/2015/04/2015-Regenerative-Capitalism-4-20-15-final.pdf> accessed 10 February 2016

in different countries. Consequently, expecting the law enforcement standard in West Africa to be exactly the same as in Western Europe is unrealistic. But it is possible to posit that law enforcement standards and practices should reflect and obey the constitutional provisions of each nation. This many will agree is a necessity minimum as most national constitutions tend to reflect the basics of universal human rights provisions, albeit with some exceptions from nation to nation.

This will inevitably lead to some variability of standards and practices, but it will be constitutionally true to each nation's landscape. So the purpose of this book is to demonstrate how law enforcement practices in Nigeria can be true to the Nigerian constitutional mandate to protect its citizens and to identify the constraints faced by the police in operationalising their constitutional obligations.

Going by the media reports on the social

media over the past few years, law enforcement has become a vital tool employed by the state to directly or indirectly violate the rights of its citizen in many African societies. The frontline law enforcement organisation in most countries is the police.

The objective of this study is to assess law enforcement governance and practices in Nigeria and suggest ways of developing and supporting good governance in its operations. This book is not about how Nigerian police can become like those in Western Europe, it is about how Nigerian police can operate within the provisions of the Nigerian constitution and legislative Acts with all its national peculiarities.

BACKGROUND TO THE STUDY

As a part of the African Union and the United Nations, Nigeria is a signatory to both the African Union and the UN Human Rights treaties. In fact, in 2009, Nigeria was the second country in Africa to deposit a national plan of action at the UN Human Rights Council. There is also domestic protection of human rights clauses incorporated into the Nigerian Constitution.

This study will seek to examine how best the police can operate within these constitutional rights provisions. It will assess the challenges and constraints faced by the Nigerian police and examine the best practices that exist in constitutional law enforcement and how these can be entrenched in Nigeria. So this book will take the form of a research study in arriving at its methodical outcomes.

QUESTIONS FOR THE STUDY

The major research questions this book seek to address are:

- What are the challenges facing the Nigerian police in its effort to promote good governance and respect for constitutional rights in its day to day operations?
- How can good governance practices

be strengthened institutionally within the Nigerian police?

- How can the promotion of constitutional rights practices facilitate effective training of law enforcement officers in Nigeria?
- What needs to be done to assist law enforcement officers to work within the nationally agreed legal and operational framework?

This study will also examine the potential impact and benefit of corrective actions such as education and of dissuasive measures such as prosecution and dismissal of offending officers on promoting and entrenching good policing and constitutional-rights focused enforcement practices in Nigeria.

OBJECTIVES OF THE STUDY

The objectives of this research are:

1) To explore the challenges facing the police (as perceived and understood

by serving, retired officers and the citizenry) in its law enforcement duties in Nigeria.

2) To explore ways this law enforcement institution can be strengthened and assisted in Nigeria.

3) To expose any institutional and structural limitations and impediments (if any) to the delivery of good policing in Nigeria.

4) To explore the use of corrective measures such as education and deterrent measures such as dismissal and prosecution of offending officers, to promote and entrench good law enforcement practices.

5) To examine ways to reduce and eradicate the real and perceived culture of impunity that seem to exist among many law enforcement officers and to explore some practices that can be deployed by the authorities to ensure a more constitutional based

human-rights compliant law enforcement operation in the country.

There have also been several reports produced by NGOs such as Human Rights Watch, Amnesty International and even the locally grown campaign group founded in 2000, NOPRIN Foundation (Network on police Reform in Nigeria), the CLEEN Foundation, just to name a few.

One thing common to most of these organisations (to a lesser extent CLEEN) is their well documented records and reports of alleged and proven abuses by the Nigeria police. It is not the intention in this research to go the same route or join issues with the findings of these organisations.

In fact, it can be agreed that they are right in many of their allegations. But this study will examine the constraints and limitations on the police in its effort to deliver on its constitutional mandate to protect the citizens. Many pages have been written on the history of law enforcement in Nigeria by several scholars over many decades.[3]

The focus of this research is to find out why the Nigerian police behave the way they do, what are the constraints or hindrances against development of good governance and respect for constitutional rights within the Nigerian police. Contextually, this study will also seek to analyse the West African regional law

---

[3] Some examples of reports, books and lectures consulted are:

1) C.D Nwankwo etal. (1993), Human Rights Practices in the Nigerian Police. Constitutional Rights Project, Lagos.
2) A.I Comassie, (1990), Discipline Superior Police Officer. A paper presented at the seminar for Area Commanders and Assistant Commissioners of Police held at the Police Staff College, Jos. March 19 -23.
3) G Ali, (2008), Police and Human Rights Abuse in Nigeria. A seminar paper presented in Department of Sociology, Ahmadu Bello University, Zaria.
4) Guelke Adrian, 2001. "Crime, Justice and the Legacy of the Past," in *Crime and Policing in Transitional Societies*. (Seminar Report). Johannesburg, RSA: Konrad Adenauer.
5) Teken Tamuno, (1989). *The Role of the Police in the Maintenance of Internal Security*. Kuru.
6) U.J.G Mohammed, (2011), Human Rights Abuses by Police Force in Bosso Police Station Minna, Niger State (unpublished Mlc project).

enforcement landscape to see what lessons can be learnt (if any).

Judging Nigerian police by Western standards will be a poor comparison as there are many contextual differences and dissimilarities to make this a credible exercise. Hence, using other West African nations to compare is a more pertinent and constructive analysis of what is possible within the environmental, socio-cultural and political context of an African society.

It was Stephen Covey who said we must *"Seek first to understand, then to be understood."*[4] If we listen first to what the genuine constraints and complaints of the Nigerian police officials are, we may better understand why they do what they do. This in no way excuses the excesses and abuses in law enforcement in Nigeria. It merely gives

---

[4] Stephen R Covey, *The Seven Habits Of Highly Effective People* (Business Library 1989).

context as to the causal factors for these behaviour.

Simply blaming and shaming the police has not changed much in the conduct of police officers as reports of abuse and misbehaviour persists. So maybe a better approach is to understand them and their challenges first, then maybe we will appreciate their constraints and they in return will better understand what society and the nation's constitution is demanding from them.

And more importantly, whether they are being adequately supported by the government and the people to fulfil the legitimate expectations of the nation.

METHODOLOGY

The focus in this study will be to understand the challenges facing the Nigerian police based on interviews conducted with the general public, retired and serving police officers, questionnaires, observation from visits to police locations, discussion with some senior politicians as well as literature reviews. This book will then seek to highlight in detail some of them.

LITERATURE REVIEW

Many handbooks,[5] articles and books have been published on the subject of Constitutional and Human Rights and Policing clearly identifying the sort of behaviour and conduct expected of law enforcement officials.

Ralf Crawshaw, Barry Revlin and Tom Williamson (1999)[6] painted a picture of the European and American model as global standard bearers in policing.

Crawshaw opined that law enforcement officials that violate the constitutional rights of

---

[5] UNHCR International Human Rights Standards for Law Enforcement, *A pocket Book on Human Rights for the police* [2004]

[6] R. Crawshaw et al *Human Rights and Policing Standards for Good Behaviour A Strategy for Change* (1999) 88.

the citizens do not make any positive contribution to the improvement of the justice system. Such violators become criminals masquerading as law officials. Such officials must be made accountable according to Crawshaw.

As part of its quest to promote best practice in this area, the United Nations produced a handbook on *Justice for Victims of Crime and Abuse of Power*,[7] in which it set clear international standards for law enforcement officials in the discharge of their lawful duties.

The thrust of the recommendations is a focus on the protection of victims and a collaborative enforcement effort by other players in the criminal justice system, as well as the local communities.

The handbook further recommended humane treatment for victims of abuse of power and

---

[7] Adopted at the UN General Assembly Resolution 40/34 29 November 1985

the prosecution of the abusers in the law enforcement community.

The brutality of the police in the Soviet Union and Eastern Europe was highlighted by Nields A Uildriks[8] as symptomatic of oppressive governments that are not accountable to their people, especially at a time of huge political transitions in the eastern bloc.

He explained the tension imposed on the police by the extreme political transition taking place while being part and subjected to the same governmental metamorphosis themselves. So this highlights how political environments can impact the policing culture and its adherence to constitutional rights standards.

Some work was produced that compiled various articles by policing players in Apartheid South Africa and its various law

---

[8] N A Uildriks *Policing Post Communist Societies: Police Public Violence, Democratic Policing And Human Rights.* (2003)7- 9.

enforcement practices from detention, bail to state of emergency. These articles were edited by Francisca Nel and Jan Bezuidenhout.[9] In Nigeria, most of the published works on policing are from historians, hence the historical thrust of these publications.

To my knowledge, no recent work has been done specifically on challenges against good governance in policing and the constitutional rights relevance of law enforcement culture in Nigeria as an academic study.

The CLEEN Foundation in Lagos have produced a few research reports on policing in Nigeria, but there is still a lot of unknown elements regarding all the constraints facing the police internally.

There has also been reports by international

---

[9] F Nel and J Bezuidenhout (eds) Policing and Human Rights (2002).

organisations such as Human Rights Watch[10] and Amnesty International on human rights abuses by the Nigerian police and military over the years.

But most of these reports are externally sourced and the police authorities in Nigeria rarely cooperate with these organisations. As with many other African countries, police in Nigeria tend to be secretive, untrusting and hostile to external scrutiny.

This may have discouraged more academic study into their practices. But with some key contacts within the Nigerian police organisation, this researcher has been able to gain unique cooperation and inside information on the operations of the law enforcement officials.

Also, the emphasis of this research is to identify the legal, cultural, capacity and

---

[10] Human Rights Watch, "Everyone's in on the Game", Corruption and Human Rights Abuses by the Nigeria Police Force (2010)

operational constraints and challenges facing the Nigerian police and how they can be best supported to be more effective and institutionally strengthened to promote good governance in law enforcement.

CONSTRAINTS

The salient challenge in conducting this research is the chronic lack of reference materials. The excitement at the start of this research was almost immediately turned into despair due to the virtual non existence of previous research materials relevant to this book. When this research topic was searched in Lexis Nexis global database, only three relevant articles came up.

This illustrates the challenge this research encountered. And within the context of Nigeria, the challenge is even more problematic.

Many of the books that are authorities on Nigerian policing were written by historians and social scientists rather than by lawyers or legal researchers.

Hence they are mostly historical accounts of the evolution of the police, pre and post independence, rather than an examination into their internal operational standards, organisational constraints and ethics. One of the main authorities whose pioneering book[11] is considered an encyclopaedia on Policing in Nigeria, Professor Emeritus T. N Tamuno, sadly passed away in April 2015 (while this research study was being finalised).

He was a Professor of History and African Studies. Access has gracefully been granted to this research to many of his published materials. However, a lot of these materials are not sociological legal writings but historical in nature.

So finding relevant current materials on the

---

[11] The police in modern Nigeria, 1861-1965: Origins, development, and role.

internal operational challenges of the Nigeria police (that is internally sourced) has been almost impossible as these are not well researched areas yet. In some respects, this research is in uncharted waters in this regard.

Several university libraries in Nigeria as well as resource centres of relevant NGOs were visited, but searches came with very little referable materials relevant to this research interest. For example, a search of all the thesis submitted in the University of Lagos from 1968-2013, revealed Zero result of a research remotely connected to this topic. So unlike many other book of this nature, there will be fewer referencing of published materials as many of the analysis are new.

Added to the above is the chronic lack of accurate and reliable data in Nigeria. Availability of facts and figures are scant and in some cases non-existent. In many of the research papers produced by the CLEEN Foundation (who have conducted much research in Nigeria on policing) the latest data produced go way back to 2008-2009 figures.

So conducting research with little or no up-to-date relevant reference materials is challenging and exciting at the same time. Exciting in that this research will be making a tangible contribution to knowledge, but challenging in that it will be a much harder work than otherwise necessary.

The foregoing will explain why there are lots of published media and newspaper references as it seems many of the key players in this arena like to give media interviews. To protect anonymity of sources, many of the facts given at interviews have not been used as they are so confidential that revealing them will inadvertently reveal their sources as well.

All the facts and stories revealed in this research from interviews have been deliberately written in such a way that will make it impossible to identify the sources.

Also, questions were asked by a few people spoken to on whether this book is a public relations or image laundering work for the police. This is not the case. The challenges faced as previously stated on getting reference materials for this research confirms the fact that many have stayed away from this area of study.

This research is therefore born out of patriotic zeal to be part of the solution rather than simply criticising the police without any constructive understanding of their operational limitations and institutional constraints.

It is hoped this study will contribute to the solution Nigeria needs in developing a constitutionally compliant police service that will fulfil its role of keeping the nation safe and people secure; while working within the rule of law.

Chapter ONE

APPROACH, FOCUS AND FINDINGS OF THE FIELD STUDY

With high youth unemployment in Nigeria, there is a high rate of crime. From murders, robbery to kidnappings and community violence exacerbated by poverty and hopelessness.

These depressing developments have made increasing numbers of Nigerians more interested in the suppression of crime and criminals and less on the methods used by the policing authorities.[12]

This study will therefore examine how police authorities in Nigeria have responded to the challenge of increasing public acceptance of violent responses by the police against perceived criminals due to the high level of violent criminality across the nation. How does this cultural push for "the ends justify the means" approach impact on the law enforcement practices and good governance in policing?

Section 194 of the 1979 Constitution of Nigeria (now Section 214 of the 1999 Constitution) gave legal effect to the modern Nigerian police force as the national police of Nigeria. The police was established to ensure internal security, to protect lives and properties of the citizens. But it faces many challenges.

---

[12] The International Council on Human Rights Policy, Crime, Public Order and Human Rights Project. Review Seminar. Carnegie Council on Ethics and International Affairs. New York, October 21-22, 2002

Questionnaires were distributed to five hundred respondents across the country and many stated what they considered as the challenges facing the police. After some analysis, this research has been able to cluster these challenges into five related groups. So for instance items relating to inadequate funding are grouped together and so on.

OVERARCHING GROUPS OF CHALLENGES

The five overarching groups are as follows:

1) *INADEQUATE FUNDING (25% of those questioned identified this as top challenge)*

Of those questioned, twenty-five percent of them believe the top challenge facing the police is related to its funding. They believe the police are not adequately funded given the size of the nation and its population.

This was identified by participants who stated the following as relating to funding challenges:

a. Inadequate Budgetary Allocation.
b. Poor Level of Pay and Conditions
c. Inadequate number of serving police personnel
d. Inadequate Operational Equipment, (Vehicles, Office Equipment, etc).
e. Poor Arms and Ammunition
f. Poor Forensic Laboratory
g. Poor Quality and Inadequate Data Bank
h. Poor Level of Intelligence Gathering and Facilities

2) *INADEQUATE PERSONNEL EDUCATION AND TRAINING (Another 25% of those interviewed identified this as a top challenge facing the police).*

This was identified by research respondents as:

a. Poor Level of Education and Quality of Majority of police

Officers

b. Ineffective and Inadequate police training regime

c. Ineffective Continuous Professional Development System

d. Effect of Breakup and Slicing-off of police Functions into multiple competing and overlapping enforcement agencies.

3) *WEAK INTERNAL GOVERNANCE, CONTROL AND DISCIPLINE. (20% of those interviewed identified this as a key challenge for the police).* This was expressed as:

a. Rampant police Corruption

b. Widespread police Abuse of suspects and citizenry

c. Lack of effective internal discipline procedure and enforcement.

d. Lack of Effective Independent complaints procedure and

accountability.

4) *INADEQUATE PUBLIC SUPPORT AND CONFIDENCE (15% of those interviewed identified this as a key challenge facing the police).* This was expressed as:

   a. Poor level of Public Support and Confidence in police

   b. Inadequate Personnel Welfare

   c. Poor Level of police Morale

   d. Excessive use of barracks to accommodate Officers, thus leading to isolation.

   e. Poor Level of Community Engagement

   f. Lack of Openness and Transparency.

   g. Excessive unrelenting Criticism by NGOs, International agencies and Nigerians.

   h. Effect of widespread abuse,

corruption and inadequacy in the wider Criminal Justice System.

5) *RELENTLESS BUT COVERT POLITICAL INTERFERENCE. (15% of those interviewed identified this as a key challenge facing the police).* This was expressed as:
   a. Political Interference in Case Management
   b. Political use of police to victimise the innocent
   c. Political use of Appointments and Internal Promotion to control senior officers
   d. Political use of inadequate Funding to control the police

To anybody that understands the workings of the Nigerian police, it will be quickly evident that the misconduct trumpeted by the media and many human rights organisations are not unconnected with a wider malady within the broader criminal justice system in Nigeria.

From the extremely slow court system, to its poor prison system and widely believed alleged judicial corruption.

These systemic weaknesses may indeed exacerbate such misbehaviour in the frontline police officers. Knowing that the wider system is corrupt may embolden wrongdoing by the frontline officers. While this book will refer to these wider factors as required to create a picture of the enabling environment, the study will however be focused only on the policing function of law enforcement.

This book (being the first volume) will not capture an in-depth treatment of the foregoing five groups of challenges as identified by the field study. So in this book our focus will be to discuss and analyse in detail only the top two groups:

- Inadequate funding and
- Poor personnel education and training

Only cursory references will be made to the other three challenge groupings as they will form the subject of a future publication by this author.

This book will also show how the development of operational excellence and respect for constitutional rights will be almost impossible unless these challenges are addressed by the Nigerian government as a matter of priority.

RESEARCH APPROACH

There are several approaches possible for Legal Research book such as this. This book has taken the Sociological approach as that include both qualitative and quantitative research methods, to look at the effect of the law in action and the part played by public policy on operationalizing the law.

It is generally believed that "*a sociological approach seeks to gain empirical knowledge and an understanding of how the law and legal proceedings impact on the parties involved. It often fills a gap in the understanding of 'law in action' found in black letter methodology perspective*"[13].

The main sources of my study will include library/desk research, materials from the Internet, media reports, extensive discussion with serving and retired Nigerian police officers, constitutional analysis of laws touching on the operations of the police, questionnaires, discussions with politicians and judicial officers, as well as observations and visits to police offices and stations.

This study will be descriptive, analytical and interactive. The starting point for this study will be as a supporter of the Nigerian police, but acting as a critical friend on identifying the Strengths, Weaknesses, Opportunities and Threats to good governance in law enforcement.

The methodology adopted also include

---

[13] 'Writing a Law Dissertation Methodology | Law Teacher' (Lawteacher.net, 2016) <http://www.lawteacher.net/law-help/dissertation/writing-law-dissertation-methodology.php#ixzz3oXVyJSu0> accessed 20 January 2016.

surveys based on questionnaires, personal interviews and as stated before library research across several institutions in Nigeria.

The questionnaire was designed with both closed and open questions in mind. Closed questions came in the ticking of boxes that best reflect the respondent's view, while open-ended questions give room for elaboration and explanation of viewpoint.

In totality, 500 questionnaires were distributed, of which 480 were returned, representing 94 percent.

Questionnaires were administered on Nigerian police officers (both serving and retired), civic leaders, personnel within the wider criminal justice system and ordinary citizens.

Also a total of twenty police locations nationwide were visited for this research. To protect the anonymity of respondents, these locations will not be identified, but they include police training facilities, police stations and detention facilities and state police command centres. Participants were selected from six states spread across all the regions of the country as follows:

No	STATE	QUESTIONEER DISTRIBUTED
1	Lagos	150
2	Abuja	150
3	Rivers	50
4	Nasarawa	50
5	Ebonyi	50
6	Sokoto	50

Figure 1: List of questionnaire distribution by state

The response rate and interest in the research in all the states visited was very good and encouraging. For those in the police, this research was seen as an overdue opportunity to get out their own side of the story. A small percentage however expressed cynicism of the value this research will bring and doubts that its findings will ever be acted upon by the authorities.

This study deliberately focuses on constitutional rights instead of simply human rights for a reason. Regardless of whether the country is signed up to International treaties on human rights, constitutional rights exists and takes primacy in Nigeria as with many other nations.

Human rights were until recently not an emphasised part of the operational agenda of the law enforcement agencies[14] in many African states and Nigeria in particular.

In addition to questionnaires, dozens of senior serving and retired police officers agreed to speak with this research. In all 120 serving and retired police officers were spoken to over a 14months period. During the field study, interviews with retired and serving police

---

[14] The Nigerian Police like many others in the sub region inherited a policing culture premised on investigative rather than preventive policing.

officers revealed an interesting trend. While 80% of the more senior officers (Commissioner rank level and above) seem to play up the successes of the police (due to existence of Policies and Procedures), 100% of the junior officers who are in the frontline believed unanimously that things are very bad and that policies and procedures are hardly implemented or operationalised.

There is evidently a clear divide between the senior and and junior officers. The overall observation (which will be developed further in this book), is that while the Nigeria police is not adequately funded by the government, the funding that exist seems to be mismanaged by the top officials of the police in a way that leaves the junior ranks with little or nothing to work with.

For instance, a Division Police Officer (DPO) who is of the Superintendent rank gave an example of the problem. He works in one of the south western states of Nigeria and was commanded to attend a training programme in the north of the country, alongside two dozen other officers of equal rank.

At the training with them were about ten Air Force officers as well. During dinner on first night, the Air Force officers explained how they were collectively given an allowance of N300,000 (about £1,000) for the four-day training.

This was a shock to the police officers in attendance. According to this DPO, he and his colleagues were not given any transport allowance to travel to and from the training venue (which was half a day travel for some) and they were not given any feeding or subsistence allowance whatsoever. They were expected to fend for themselves, while attending a compulsory training.

The question the DPO then asked was, *"How do I find the money to go on this training, unless I collect bribes from the general public?"*. His monthly salary was N150,000 (about £500). Out of which he claims N50,000 is deducted for police Pension contribution. He has a wife and six children.

But when speaking with a more senior officer at the police headquarters, it was stated that there were allocations for officers to attend such training as a matter of policy. So the allocation disappeared somewhere between the headquarters and the state police commanders.

This is typical of many stories this research was told by frustrated junior officers, who have nothing but contempt for their superiors who they believe corruptly steal the already inadequate allocations that exist, thus leaving them with no choice but to collect bribes to survive.

Another DPO interviewed narrated an additional example of this divide. This DPO said one of his team was killed in line of duty three months earlier. The late officer was survived by wife and four children. This DPO almost weeping stated that he had to levy all the officers in his division with a contribution to enable the family to take the deceased officer's body to his village for burial and to give some funds to the family.

When asked about the much announced police pension and insurance schemes, he laughed. He stated that in many cases, these are never paid out and if they do, it takes months if not years.

"*Do they expect the corpses not to be buried for months?*" he asked sarcastically. So here again we see a divide between theoretical policies and procedures that senior officers claim exists and reality of poor or inadequate implementation on the frontline.

This field study encountered dozens of similar stories by the junior officers interviewed across many states in Nigeria. Their revealing insights will shape many of the recommendations in this book.

FIELD STUDY AND SUMMARY QUESTIONNAIRE FINDINGS

For this research, fifty interviews were conducted with serving and retired police officers with 70% being of senior rank of chief superintendent and above.

For the questionnaire distribution, a 60:40 approach was taken. That is 60% of participants were serving or retired police officers, mostly of lower to middle ranking, (from new recruits to chief superintendents). And 40% were members of the public, community leaders and workers in the criminal justice system.

So in every state where the questionnaire was distributed, the above distribution formulae was used.

This approach was informed by the fact that there are plenty of media reports on how badly the general public regard the police, but there is no research that could be found on how the police regard themselves if given a neutral and anonymised opportunity to respond.

The goal is not just to reveal what the public think of the police, but more importantly what the police think of the police if given assurance of confidentiality. The result is astonishing.

The research shows that police officers, mirrors the public opinion substantially in terms of judgement on low performance and ineffectiveness of the police.

This reveals a level of self awareness that many thought did not exist within the police.

Below are sample summary of participants responses to key questions:

KEY QUESTION ASKED	% with Little or No Confidence (Among Police – Serving or Retired)	% with Little or No Confidence (Among the General Public)
Overall how much confidence do you have in the Nigerian Police?	80%	100%

Figure 2 : Sample Question 1

	KEY QUESTION ASKED	% with Dissatisfied or Very Dissatisfied response (Among Police – Serving or Retired)	% with Dissatisfied or Very Dissatisfied response (Among the General Public)
	How satisfied are you with Nigerian police performance in Investigating Crime?	70%	98%

Figure 3 : Sample Question 2

KEY QUESTION ASKED	% with Dissatisfied or Very Dissatisfied (Among Police – Serving or Retired)	% with Dissatisfied or Very Dissatisfied (Among the General Public)
How satisfied are you with Nigerian police performance in addressing Crime Prevention?	95%	100%

Figure 4 : Sample Question 3

	KEY QUESTION ASKED	% that says Not Effective (Among Police – Serving or Retired)	% that says Not Effective (Among the General Public)
	In general, how effective do you believe the Police is in providing services to your community?	80%	100%

Figure 5 : Sample Question 4

KEY QUESTION OR STATEMENT ASKED	% that Disagree or Strongly Disagree (Among Police – Serving or Retired)	% that Disagree or Strongly Disagree (Among the General Public)
Nigerian police is accountable to the public?	85%	100%

Figure 6 : Sample Question 5

When asked, what are the *"obstacles to you dealing with the Police in your day to day life"*, forty percent of the general public stated they were afraid to get involved with the police.

Another thirty percent cited police corruption

as the barrier for them. Some five percent said they assumed the police will do nothing.

Lack of police response or action in the past and the time consuming nature of reporting and engaging with the police was cited by another twenty percent. More results of the interviews with senior police officers will be revealed as applicable in future chapters of this book.

BOOK CHAPTER BREAKDOWN

In addition to my Introduction section, the book is divided into six Chapters as follows:

> ➢ Chapter ONE - APPROACH AND FOCUS OF THE FIELD RESEARCH

> ➢ Chapter TWO - HISTORICAL AND CURRENT OVERVIEW OF CONSTITUTIONAL ROLE OF POLICING IN NIGERIA

> ➢ Chapter THREE - OVERVIEW OF

POLICING IN SUB SAHARAN AFRICA

- ➤ Chapter FOUR - FUNDING CHALLENGES FACING THE NIGERIA POLICE

- ➤ Chapter FIVE - CHALLENGES OF PERSONNEL EDUCATION and TRAINING FACING THE NIGERIA POLICE

- ➤ Chapter SIX - RECOMMENDATIONS FOR DEVELOPING GOOD GOVERNANCE IN THE NIGERIA POLICE

The dominant approach is to create a progression of analysis in this book. After the Introduction has captured the basis of the research and its objectives, the study then proceeds to explain the approach to and focus of the field and desk research conducted.

In Chapter Two, the book explains the

historical and current overview of the constitutional framework as well as operational structures of the Nigeria police. From a brief history of the creation of the police to the current operational structure as well as oversight arrangements. Chapter Three captures a summarised view of policing in ECOWAS region identifying common elements and challenges while making some recommendations.

However, Chapters Four and Five deals with the two areas of focus of this research in detail. Finally, the book is concluded in Chapter Six with recommendations for developing good governance in Nigeria police as related to the primary areas of focus.

Supporting Good Governance in the Nigerian Police Force.

Chapter TWO

HISTORICAL PERSPECTIVES, POWERS AND ORGANISATIONAL STRUCTURE OF POLICE IN NIGERIA

In historical African societies, policing was the job of all adults in village communities. Under the system of 'Hue, Cry and Pursuit' adults in communities were expected to be involved in control and crime prevention under the leadership of village and tribal elders.

But the emergence of the State structure with

its vast bureaucracies and grasp for power, hierarchy and control changed the entrenched convention that policing is everybody's job.

There are several historical versions of the evolution of the Nigeria police, but the central theme in these available materials relates to the strong-arm tactics of the colonial regime which required a ruthless force to deal with restless locals in order to enable ease of management of Nigeria as a colony.

Sir Stanhope Freeman, as the Governor of British West Africa, is generally credited with the foresight and initiative that created the initial group that later transformed into the police force of Nigeria[15]. Nwanze, posited:

> "Sir Freeman wrote a memo to the British Home Office requesting authority to create a force different from the Army to act as consular guards. His

---

[15] Sam Nwanze, "In Thy Hands oh God: The Man, the Cop, the Preacher", Nio Publishers Lagos, 1999. P.79

request was granted and the force, which he formed, was used to quell the Epe uprising of 1863. The activities of the guards drew the attention of the Governor of Lagos Colony, Captain John Glover. It was Captain Glover who requested and received permission of London to increase the number of the force to one hundred. Shortly after, the "Hausa Guard" and the Constabulary of the Lagos Colony were established. A legal instrument backed the new forces as an ordinance was enacted in 1879. This law was however amended with another ordinance, which created the Lagos Police Force, an investigative unit known as the criminal investigative department, in 1896".[16]

In his recorded account Tamuno[17] says that the Nigerian police originated between 1845

---

[16] ibid
[17] Tekena Tamuno, The Police in Modern Nigeria 1861-1965, University Press Ibadan, 1970

and 1861. With the colonial power's need for centralised control and compliance, a professionalised policing ethos was established to exert the state control, with or without the consent of the people. In those days there were no distinction between the police and the military tactics when it came to the exertion of state hegemony and dominance. This created a militarised policing culture that has remained in many African societies till date.

According to Weber 1968,[18] the state gained the monopoly of legitimate violence and its delivery agents through the police in many nations, which in the case of African societies it was the continued colonial rule.

Hence the police operated to secure the interest of the colonisers and not that of the colonised. This 'ruling class' focus of the early police organisation in Nigeria during the

---

[18] Weber, M. (1968) *Economy and Society,* university of California Press

colonial era, many will say has not really changed in the post-colonial period.

Although its powers and operations are defined by laws, the practical operations of the police is affected by the political and socio-economic interests of the governing elite and political groups in many nations. This fact was emphasised by Robert Reiner when he stated:

> "The police are the specialist carriers of the state's bedrock power: the monopoly of legitimate use of force. How and for what this is used speaks to the very heart of the condition of a political order. The danger of abuse, on behalf of particular partisan interests or the police themselves are clear and daunting".[19]

---

[19] Robert Reiner (1993) "Police Accountability: Principles, Patterns and Practices" in R. Reiner and S. Spencer (eds.) *Accountability Policing: Effectiveness, Empowerment and Equity* (London: Institute of public Policy Research).

Hence it is posited that the more democratic a state is, the better the police will be at operating in the interest of the many rather than the few. As the police is a reflection of the state that controls it, an undemocratic state will be more oppressively policed for the benefit of the few.

So operational excellence in policing is easier in a state with advanced and developed democratic institutions and paradigm. Police were used by the colonial masters to brutally supress any opposition by the locals all over Nigeria. This started the negative perception of the police by Nigerians, a situation that has not changed after independence.

After securing home rule from the British in 1960, many expected a wholesome reorganisation of the police and its operating legal framework. That did not happen.

Instead a merely ceremonial transfer of service to local political leaders took place, leaving all the colonial statutes, ethos and legislative framework in place. This reality was left unchanged and some may say even made worse with decades of military dictatorships.

After independence, the Nigerian government accelerated the process of centralisation of the police, doing away with regional forces who were seen as badly trained, corrupt and political tools for local leaders.

So since the 1979 Constitution, there has been a provision for a national police force for the Nigerian state controlled from the centre. This was again affirmed in the 1999 Constitution.[20]

So the Nigerian state maintains a federal unified national police structure with each of the thirty-six states and Federal Capital City (FCT) Abuja having a police command led by a commissioner but controlled by the national leadership of the force.

---

[20] Section 214(1)

POLICE POWERS AND LAWFUL FUNCTIONS

The duties and powers of the police are well articulated in the Police Act, 1943. Section 4 of the Act itemised the basic duties of the police as directly quoted below:[21]

- prevention and detection of crime
- apprehension of offenders
- preservation of law and order
- due enforcement of all laws and regulations with which they are directly, charged, and
- The performance of such other military duties within or outside Nigeria as may be required of them by or under the authority of the Act or any other Act. [22]

Additional powers and constitutional duties of the police included in the Act are:

- Power to conduct prosecutions in any court, subject to constitutional provision relating to the power of the

---

[21] ibid
[22] ibid

Attorney-General of the Federation and of a state[23].

- Power to arrest without warrant in possession[24].
- Power to serve summons[25].
- Power to grant bail to a person arrested without warrant[26].
- Power to issue search warrant by a superior officer[27].
- Power to take and record for purpose of identification and measurement, photographs and finger prints

With police powers comes responsibility as well. This is not different in Nigeria. Section 298 of the Criminal Procedure Code states that:

"any person authorized by law to use force is criminally responsible for any excess according to the nature and

---

[23] S.25 of the Police Act
[24] ibid
[25] S.26 of the Police Act
[26] S.27 of the Police Act
[27] S.28 of the Police Act

quality of the act which is the excess"[28]

Additionally Section 374 (a,b) of the Police Regulations of 1968 allows for judicial oversight of police use of its powers.

Section 4 of the Police Act states that:
"The police shall be employed for the prevention and detection of crime, the apprehension of offenders, the preservation of law and order, the protection of life and property and the due enforcement of all laws and regulations with which they are charged and shall perform such military duties within or without Nigeria as may be required...[29]"

So the police in Nigeria are empowered by law to carry out global standard policing duties and enforcement of the law and keeping of the peace. With mass poverty and high unemployment in Nigeria, along with the many operational challenges facing the police that is

---

[28] The Criminal Procedure Code of Nigeria
[29] ibid

being examined in this book, police are seen as serving only the rich and powerful. They provide personal security to the rich and highly connected while the poor are largely left to fend for themselves and unprotected.

Many of the operational challenges this research found makes it easier and some will say inevitable for the police to become subservient to the rich and powerful. And some may say it seems to be in the interest of the ruling class to keep things the way they are as it entrenches their hegemony and control of the nation's resources.

The 1999 Constitution of the Federal Republic of Nigeria in section 214 (1) states that:
"There shall be a Police Force for Nigeria, which shall be known as the Nigeria Police Force and subject to the provisions of this section, no other Police Force shall be established for the Federation or any part thereof".

Section 214 (2)(a) empowers the National

Assembly to produce an Act to organize and administer the details of police operations in Nigeria in ways that protects the constitutional rights of Nigerians. This is known as the Police Act. First enacted in 1943, it has been reviewed by the legislature in 1967 and 1979. A new review is being planned by the National Assembly.

This constitutional provision makes it unconstitutional for either the government of the states or even the federal government to establish a parallel police service in competition to the Nigeria police Force. This has however not stopped the Federal government from establishing additional investigatory and enforcement institutions, even though they have not called any of them 'police'.

Senior government officials and ninety percent of senior police officers interviewed by this research agree that the Nigerian government seem to be in breach of the spirit of the constitution if not the letter of it. By not calling these parallel agencies "police" the government seem to say they have stayed within the provisions of the law. But with these agencies having powers similar to that of the police, it can be argued that if it looks like a dog, barks like a dog, walks like a dog, then it is a dog.

These agencies perform policing duties, hence in can be argued that they are police in practice if not in names. But nobody has yet litigated this fact by taking the government to court of competent jurisdiction over it. Examples of these additional agencies are:

- The Federal Road Safety Commission (FRSC)
- The Economic and Financial Crime Commission (EFCC)
- The Independent Corrupt Practices Commission (ICPC)
- The National Civil Defence Corps (NCDC)
- The Code of Conduct Bureau (CCB)
- Vehicle Inspection Office

- Code of Conduct Tribunal (CCT)
- State Security Service (SSS)
- National Drug Law Enforcement Agency (NDLEA)

For instance, the CCT has not led to accelerated hearings of misconduct cases, hence there is doubt as to its continued existence. But this will be dealt with in Chapter Six.

One hundred percent of the senior police officers interviewed believe the plethora of agencies, many with overlapping powers, has led to the weakening of the main police force as a result of talent flight to these agencies and reduction in police funding, as funds are allocated to these additional agencies.

The main police force is then left to do the heavy lifting task of crime prevention and investigation with less resources to do the job. We will examine these policing agencies impact on core police funding later in this book. These policing related agencies consume a lot of resources and those questioned for this study believe overwhelmingly they are inefficient and incoherent in operational agility.

Legally speaking, the operations of the police are administered by a myriad of colonial acts, decrees, the Constitution, the Police Act and others.

The full list of governing instruments of the police are:
  i.   The Nigerian Constitution,
  ii.   The Public Service Rules,
  iii. The Police Service Commission Establishment Act 2001.
  iv.   The Police Standing Orders
  v.   The Police Act and Regulations
  vi.   The Financial Regulations
  vii. The Force Orders
  viii. The Force CID Circulars.
  ix.   The Force Administrative Instructions,

In many other countries, there is only the main

police force, with divisions and specialised units and branches to deal with particular crimes. For some inexplicable reason, the governments of Nigeria over the past thirty years established these parallel agencies some with dubious, conflicting and confusing mandates.

Based on Section 4 of the Nigerian Police Act 1943 as earlier quoted, the police are adequately empowered to enforce all laws and rights of citizens as provided by the Nigerian Constitution and other Acts of the National Assembly.

It is the objective of this book to show how the police can be supported in delivering its constitutional duties via effective and good institutional governance.

Chapter IV of the Nigerian 1999 Constitution (as amended) lists the fundamental rights of the citizens. These are similar to the European Charter of Fundamental and Human Rights, which reflects the provisions of the United Nation's Universal Declaration of Human rights. In summary these rights are stated in the Nigerian as follows:

i.   Right to Life[30]

ii.   Right to Respect for the dignity of a person[31]

iii.   Right to Personal Liberty[32]

iv.   Right to Fair Hearing[33]

v.   Right to Private and Family Life[34]

vi.   Right to Freedom of thought, conscience and religion[35]

vii.   Right to Freedom of expression at the Press[36]

viii.   Right to Peaceful assembly and association[37]

ix.   Right to Freedom of movement[38]

x.   Right to Freedom from discrimination[39]

xi.   Right to Acquire and own immovable property anywhere in Nigeria[40]

---

[30] Chapter IV, Section 33 (1) of the Nigerian constitution
[31] Section 34 (1) of the Nigerian Constitution
[32] Section 35 (1) of the Nigerian Constitution
[33] Section 36 (1) of the Nigerian Constitution
[34] Section 37 of the Nigerian Constitution
[35] Section 38 (1) of the Nigerian Constitution
[36] Section 39 (1) of the Nigerian constitution
[37] Section 40 of the Nigerian constitution
[38] Section 41 (1) of the Nigerian constitution
[39] Section 42 (1) of the Nigerian constitution
[40] Section 43 of the Nigerian Constitution

POLICE UNDER MILITARY GOVERNMENTS

In a functioning democracy, policing is usually by consent of the citizens. They count on the goodwill and cooperation of the public in carrying out their duties. The Nigerian police with its militarised colonial origin and decades of military rule have become alienated from the people and seen merely as an oppressive tool in the hands of government.

For most of its years since Independence, Nigeria was ruled by the Military through the various coups that took place. This reality had a devastating and regressive impact on the police.

After the military coup of 1966, the military co-opted the police into government by making two of their ranks Governors. According to Asemota,[41] the Military needed the police

---

[41] S.A Asemota . Policing Under Civilian and Military Administrations". in Policing Nigeria, Past, Present and Future, (eds.) Tekena Tamuno et al, Malthouse Press

after the 1966 coup as the police were the only institution that had communication links all over Nigeria and had presence in every town in the country. Hence cooperation of the police was required to sustain the military rule, especially given that at that time the army was very small in comparison to the population.

The emergence of police officers as governors began the blurring of lines between the arms of government, thus the disappearance of the normal checks and balances expected. But this is typical of undemocratic military government which was what Nigeria had from 1966 up till 1979 when there was four years of democracy that was again truncated by another military coup.

Coming out of the civil war strengthened in number and infrastructure, the military felt they no longer need the police. So after the

---

Limited Lagos 1993, page 397.

coup that brought General Murtala Mohammed into power, the police were no longer represented at all in government. This reality many believe was the beginning of the modern neglect of the police.

It has been argued by some, even within the police in Nigeria that the previous military governments that ruled Nigeria for more than half of its Independent years, made deliberate efforts to emasculate and disempower the police.

This many argue was intended to ensure the police did not develop the competence, number and capability to challenge the military through the many coups that brought the army into power.

A salient champion of this school of thought was a police Public Relations Officer for Lagos state during the Babangida military regime in the 1980s, who was suspended and dismissed[42] due to his "radical" claim of the disempowerment of the police by the military juntas. His name is Alozie Ogubuaja.

According to Ogubuaja:

> "A military government will want a weak police force so that they can twist them as they want. The military want a weak police so that they can be used to do their biddings, the good, the bad and the ugly. Secondly, a weak and inefficient police force raises the profile of the military as masters in power. Thirdly, a strong and efficient police force is a threat to the military because there can not be two captains in one ship. The military would want a monopoly of power, to dominate and rule".[43]

His views are widely shared by many in

---

[42] He was dismissed in 1988 from the Nigeria Police Force by the military rulers
[43] <https://groups.yahoo.com/neo/groups/NIgerianWorldForu m/conversations/messages/42023> accessed 12 January 2016

Nigeria. This has made him a hero to many who want a better and accountable police force in Nigeria.

A consequence of this prevalent view is the increased distrust of the police senior hierarchy who are seen as weak and conniving with the government of the day for pecuniary gain but to the detriment of the frontline officers in the police. The mistrust and even hatred for the police was made worse during the decades of military rule.

The police were used to enforce unpopular and draconian decrees, which further alienated them from the people. Policing in Nigeria has never been by popular consent of the citizens, but by fear and force and sometimes brutal force.

So when the police become the enforcement agents for unpopular and undemocratic governance and rules, they will suffer from the understandable hatred of and opprobrium directed at the government in charge.

While the military when in power invested and modernise themselves infrastructure wise, the police was largely under funded and neglected. But the continuing negative public perception of the role and capacity of the police is a major source of concern in a democracy.

Hence the police remain the most misunderstood profession by the general public in Nigeria. Many expect them to work magic despite the limitations and constraints of their tools and service conditions. Their performance is weighed with misconception and ignorance, resulting in an out of context assessment of their activities.

Ignorance of the inner workings of the police and the penchant for secrecy by the Nigeria police had led to little public confidence in the service, plenty of misconception and depleted public support and cooperation with the police.

As already stated, the Nigeria police are

saddled with the constitutional responsibilities of prevention and detection of crime. They are also expected to perform *"such military duties within or without Nigeria as may be required of them by or under the authority of this or any other act*[44]'. This means there is a Military and Non-Military duties expected of the police.

The non military duties are interwoven in the sense that the prevention and detection of crime amounts to preservation of law and order and protection of life and property.[45] This is their law enforcement duties.

Within this is the role of the police as criminal justice administrators from investigation to bringing prosecution and enforcement of the courts judgements. Their military related role involve both international security deployments via the United Nations, African

---

[44] Section 4 Police Act. Cap 359, Laws of the Federation of Nigeria 1990

[45] A Adeyemi, Police and Human Rights in a Democratic Nigeria. A Paper on Human Rights and Law Enforcement in Nigeria. (2005) p.37 Edited by S.G Ehindero and E.E.O Alemika

Union or ECOWAS as well as domestic enforcement duties.

Given the foregoing pivotal and all encompassing roles they play, the police have become a key institution for social order in Nigeria. Since no law operates in vacuum, police enforcement gives value to the law and helps to regulate traditional tension between the antagonistic forces inherent in Nigerian and all human societies.

From colonial era, through military rule and the democratic dispensation, policing in Nigeria has been a tough task.

Conflicts arising from social inequalities, political, religious and cultural differences appear to have widened the role and function of the police beyond the traditional law enforcement to other social services functions. So police are working in tense environments, in which their actions or inactions can have national ramifications.

However, the Nigeria police has been under lots of public criticism, especially since the late 70s over its apparent inability to effectively prevent or control crime. Several factors have been attributed to this sorry state of affairs. Some of the key complaints are:

- Lack of professionalism, generally attributed to the recruitment policy which has on the quality of manpower.

- Poor training and institutional lack of discipline.

- Corruption and culture of bribe taking.

- Low number of manpower and poor equipment.

- Bribe collection to work against the interest of justice. The highest bribe payers tend to get the police to support their position.

A few of these will be explored later, but the consequence of these institutional problems is the resulting distrust and poor image and regard for the police by the citizenry.

ORGANISATIONAL STRUCTURE OF THE POLICE

There has been various iteration of changes to the police force in Nigeria since its centralisation. While not dwelling on the historical element, it is prudent to explain the current structure. Nigeria comprises of 36 States and the Federal Capital Territory (FCT) named Abuja.

The force is now managed under, **A, B, C, D, E and F** departments (plus a new department for ICT) with Deputy Inspectors General (DIG) in command.

With six new states created in 1996, the zonal command structure was reformed to Twelve zones with an Assistant Inspector General (AIG) in charge.

The zoning is as follows:

ZONE No	STATE COMMAND
Zone 1	Kano, Jigawa, Katsina
Zone 2	Lagos, Ogun
Zone 3	Adamawa, Gombe, Taraba
Zone 4	Benue, Plateau, Nassarawa
Zone 5	Edo, Delta, Bayelsa
Zone 6	Rivers, Ebonyi, C/River, Akwa Ibom
Zone 7	Niger, Kaduna, FCT
Zone 8	Kogi, Kwara, Ekiti,
Zone 9	Abia, Anambra, Enugu, Imo
Zone 10	Kebbi, Sokoto, Zamfara
Zone 11	Ondo, Osun, Oyo
Zone 12	Bauchi, Borno, Yobe

Figure 7 : Zoning of Police formations[46]

---

[46] 'Home Page - Nigeria Police Force' (Npf.gov.ng, 2016) <http://www.npf.gov.ng/> accessed 11 November 2015

The AIG in charge of the zones as well as Commissioners for each state get reassigned so frequently that there is no point listing their names. There has been period where officers were moved around up to four times within a year.

The Departments and their duties as stated by the Nigerian police website[47] are as follows:

DEPARTMENT A
- Administration.
- Personnel- Promotion, dismissal, transfer and posting.
- Welfare
- Budgeting, finance, pay and accounts.
- Establishment
- Medical.
- Public Relations / printing.
- Computers.
- Central band.
- Cooperative.
- Force Provost.

---

[47] ibid

- Central Motor Registry.
- Supernumerary constable, special constabulary.

DEPARTMENT B

- Operation - Joint operation, Highway patrol, Motor, Traffic Warden service, Motor Traffic Control and Policies.
- Airport, Railway and Ports Authority police.
- Central motor Registry.
- Force Armament - Arms and Ammunition, Musketry, Bomb Disposal, Anti
- Terrorism.
- Police mobile force and training college.
- Transport, Air-wing.
- Signals - communication.
- Force Animals - Mounted Section, Dogs and Veterinary.

DEPARTMENT C

- Works, Building, Engineering and Maintenance.
- Supplies/Stores Stationery, Office Equipment, Kits and Accoutrements.
- Procurement Tender Boards.
- Board of Survey for Vehicle and Unserviceable store.

DEPARTMENT D

- General investigation.
- International police.
- Antiquities.
- Crime prevention.
  Technical aid to criminal investigation, forensic laboratory, criminal records, central arms registry, photography and etching sections.
- Legal section -legal advice, criminal prosecution, civil litigation, library, and administration.
- Criminal intelligence Bureau.
- Security intelligence Bureau.
- Squad.
- Special Fraud Unit / Failed Bank

Inquiries
- Special Anti - Robbery Squad.
- Homicide.

Department E
- Training.
- Police Academy.
- Police staff college.
- Police colleges at Ikeja, Kaduna, Maiduguri Oji River and Detective College
- Enugu
- Education -local and Overseas.

Department F
- Research.
- Planning.
- Inspectorate Division.
- Management Information.
- Organization and method.

ICT Department

National Operational Structure

The Inspector General of police administers both the Force Headquarters management and also the Zonal command structures.

Figure 8 : National Police Headquarters Structure

Section 215 (1) (A) of the 1999 Constitution as amended states as follows:

> "An Inspector-General of Police who, subject to section 216(2) of this Constitution, shall be appointed by the President on the advice of the Nigeria Police Council from among serving members of the Nigeria Police Force".

All the senior police officers interviewed confirmed that the Nigeria Police Council (NPC) have met only once the past decade. The NPC consists of the President and all the state governors as the minister in charge of Abuja the federal capital, the IGP himself and the chairman of the Police Service Commission.

The NPC has long been considered a statutory but redundant body that never meet, thus given the President a complete discretion on when to dismiss or appoint an Inspector General of Police.

Hence the IG remains in office essentially based on the President's prerogative. This situation can create possible pressure on the IG to tow the presidential political line or be dismissed. The independence of the IG is doubtful under this circumstances.

Nigeria has had ten Inspector Generals of Police (IGP) in ten years. There is no security of tenure and they are hired and fired by the

President at his leisure, thanks to a redundant NPC. Despite the constitutional clause[48] requiring that the President consult the NPC before hiring or removing an IGP, this never happen in practice claimed a hundred percent of senior police officers interviewed.

The Constitution[49] also states that an IGP must be a serving police officer, thus restricting the pool of available candidates to those already within the polluted police system.

Therefore, at the head of the Nigeria police hierarchy is the Inspector General of Police (IGP). Despite the Constitutional mandate for consultation with NPC to take place, the holder of this post is an appointee of the President. He is consequently serving at the pleasure of the President of Nigeria.

---

[48] Section 216 (2) of the 1999 Constitution of Nigeria as amended
[49] Section 215 (1) (A) of the 1999 Constitution of Nigeria as amended

At the Force headquarters, reporting to the IGP are six Deputy Inspector General of police (DIG) who are in charge of the the six departments as noted above. There is also an official in charge of the ICT department but not a DIG rank.

The Constitution in a sort of contradictory way mandates that the IGP must obey all lawful instructions of the President. Section 215 (3) of the 1999 Constitution states as follows:

> "The President or such other Minister of the Government of the Federation as he may authorise in that behalf may give to the Inspector-General of Police such lawful directions with respect to the maintenance and securing of public safety and public order as he may consider necessary, and the Inspector-General of Police shall comply with those directions or cause them to be compiled with".[50]

---

[50] ibid

But the Constitution does not give any avenue or option to the IGP to appeal or seek judicial review of any instruction he perceives as unlawful. This creates a strong case for constitutional amendment to provide a channel for the IGP to challenge an unlawful direction from the President. This will be addressed in Chapter Six of this book as part of reform recommendations.

Currently, Section 215 (5) of the Constitution closes down this possibility by stating as follows:

> "The question whether any, and if so what, directions have been given under this section shall not be inquired into in any court".[51]

This section is open to interpretations. Some might say that the section only prevents the disclosure of the content of an order to the IGP. But there is no constitutionally stated procedure for the IGP to seek review of any

---

[51] ibid

perceived unlawful order from the president. Also the lawfulness of an order cannot be determined without the content of the order being revealed [which will breach Section 215 (5)]. So this leaves the IGP with no real choice but to obey all orders of the President or resign.

If the IGP thinks a direction from the President is unlawful, there is no avenue for him or her to appeal or context the direction independently. This anomaly is one of the ways the political leadership exert control over the IGP and the entire police force.

Zonal Structure

Nigeria is divided into twelve zones. Each zone comprises of a mixture of between two to four states, each commanded by an AIG.

The Zones are grouped together based on several factors such as population density, crime statistics, property volume, level of economic activities and so on. That is why some zones have two states while others have up to four.

Figure 9 : Organisation of police zonal commands

State Structure

Each state is led by a Commissioner of Police (CP). The commissioner post is enshrined in the Constitution, just like the IGP post. Each state is then divided into Units, Divisions and Areas, which are led by officers of different ranks.

Section 215 (1) (b) of the Constitution states as follows:

> "A Commissioner of Police for each state of the Federation who shall be appointed by the Police Service Commission'.[52]

---

[52] ibid

It is arguable if a body such as the Police Service Commission is needed to appoint commissioners.

An independent board under the police headquarters with fifty percent independent members should be able to perform this role; thus saving the country money. This will be addressed specially under the recommendations in Chapter Six.

In professional policing, the rank of the Commissioner is the highest professional rank an officer can attain. This is also technically the same in Nigeria. However, the institutional system in Nigeria provides for three additional ranks above that of the Commissioner. These are:

- Assistant Inspector General of Police (AIG)
- Deputy Inspector General of Police (DIG)
- Inspector General of Police (IGP).

It is well accepted knowledge that the ranks above that of the Commissioner are largely political posts and lots of politics is played at this level. I do not mean party politics in the traditional sense, but a lot of governmental and political considerations comes to prominence much more at these levels.

POLICE OVERSIGHT BODIES

Section 4 of the Police Act as previously noted states the basic duties of the police in Nigeria. Nigeria police Force is a centralised organisation with the Inspector General (IG) at the top of the hierarchy.

There are constitutional bodies with the mandate to supervise and manage the operations of police in Nigeria. The main bodies are:
- The Ministry of Police Affairs
- The Police Service Commission
- The Senate committee on police affairs (the committee's role is less operational but more persuasive)

Ministry of Police Affairs

Based on its own website, the Ministry declares its role as being:

> "charged with responsibility of overseeing the affairs of the Nigeria Police Force and officers and men of the Police Force. The Ministry is unique when compared to other Ministries on the basis of its statutory mandate as enshrined in sections 5, 147 and 148 of the Constitution of the Federal Republic of Nigeria which include formulating policies and provide administrative support for the ministry, the police council and the Nigeria police, oversee the training and welfare matters of the police, police Pensions Administration, and any other matters as may be assigned by the President, Commander-in-Chief of the Armed Forces and chairman Nigeria police Council".[53]

---

[53]'Ministry Of Police Affairs • Brief History' (Policeaffairs.gov.ng, 2016)

With many departments replicating those within the police headquarters, It is questionable what value added this big bureaucracy brings to the operation of the police, especially given the mandate of the next oversight organisation.

Police Service Commission

The Police Service Commission (PSC) is a child of the 1957 Constitutional Conference but was not established until 2001. This was due to decades of military rule in Nigeria which saw the repeated suspension of the democratic Constitution as the military ruled by decrees. The nation's current democratic resurgence started in 1999, hence the PSC came into full existence in 2001.

PSC is an Independent Government Agency *"established by Section 153 of the 1999 Constitution with the power to Appoint, Promote, Post, Dismiss and exercise*

<http://www.policeaffairs.gov.ng/about-us/brief-history> accessed 11 January 2016.

disciplinary control over members of the Nigeria police Force".[54]

Paragraph 30 of Schedule 3 to the 1999 Constitution of Nigeria states as follows:

The Commission has the power to:-

a) appoint persons to offices (other than the office of the Inspector-General of Police) in the Nigeria Police Force, and[55]

b) dismiss and exercise disciplinary control over persons holding any office referred to in sub-paragraph (a) of this paragraph.[56]

The Commission has power over all officers of the Nigeria police, except the IGP. Additionally, Section 215 (1) (b) states: *"There shall be a Commissioner of Police for each State of the Federation who shall be appointed by the Police Service*

---

[54] 'Index Of /' (Psc.gov.ng, 2016) <http://www.psc.gov.ng/> accessed 11 January 2016

[55] The Nigerian 1999 Constitution

[56] ibid

Commission".[57] A secondary instrument also gives legal basis for its operations. This is the police Service Commission (Establishment, etc) Act, 2001.

Part II (6) also states that the Commission shall be responsible to:[58]

- Appoint and promote persons to offices (other than the office of the Inspector-General of police) in the Nigeria Police Force,[59]

- Dismiss and exercise disciplinary control over persons (other than the Inspector-General of Police) in the Nigeria Police Force,[60]

- Formulate policies and guidelines for the appointment, promotion, discipline and dismissal of Officers of the Nigeria

---

[57] Extract from the Nigerian 1999 Constitution as amended
[58] 'Index Of /' (Psc.gov.ng, 2016) <http://www.psc.gov.ng/> accessed 11 January 2016
[59] ibid
[60] ibid

Police Force,[61]

- Identify factors inhibiting or undermining discipline in the Nigeria Police Force,[62]

- Formulate and implement policies aimed at the efficiency and discipline of the Nigeria Police Force,[63]

- Delegate powers to any Member or Committee of members of the Nigeria Police Force it may deem fit.[64]

- Implement directives which may from time to time be given by the President.[65]

Ninety percent of the police officers interviewed believe that these two bodies should be scrapped. This author agrees. With duplicated roles and bureaucratic bottlenecks created, in a country like Nigeria, this gives

---

[61] ibid
[62] ibid
[63] ibid
[64] ibid
[65] ibid

much room for corruption as too many officials need to sanction each activity or procurement.

This is one of the key reasons why the already inadequate police budgetary allocations get mismanaged at the top with frontline officers complaining of never receiving promised equipment or allocations.

It is reasonable to suggest that these two should be merged and streamlined. For the police to secure operational independence, the oversight at the federal level should be scaled down and those at the state and local level enhanced to ensure effective local and state accountability. The attempts made to speak with the PSC were unsuccessful during this research.

Senate Committee on Police Affairs

This is a standing committee of the Nigerian Senate with focus on police affairs. They do not have any direct special powers, but can investigate any matters relating to the police, hold enquiries and report their findings with recommendations to the full chamber.

Action available to the committee could be simply drawing attention to special areas or issues relating to policing to recommending legislative changes to the Police Act or even the Constitution. The Committee does not have direct powers currently in relation to the appointment or dismissal of the IGP.

Chapter THREE

OVERVIEW OF POLICING IN WEST AFRICA

A regional analysis is helpful in contextualizing the challenges facing the Nigerian police and it is a good starting point to create a baseline picture of the tasks facing policing in Nigeria. Any discussion on the development of operational excellence in policing in Nigeria will have to examine both the constitutional rights of the citizens as well as that of police officers on duty.

This will require an examination of both the obligation of the State to support and equip the police as well as the duty on the policy to uphold constitutional rights of citizens while carrying out their duties.

There are various frameworks that exist to guide the operational activities of police authorities around the world, but they all have common threads within them. The role of the African Commission on Human and Peoples' Rights (ACHPR) as it relates to police matters is based on the African Charter on the same subject matter.

Member states agree to give recognition to the freedoms expressed in the said Charter and '*undertake to adopt legislative and other measures to give effect to them*'.[66] The Economic Community of West African States (ECOWAS) code of conduct is adopted the same principles. The operationalizing of this code is however a challenge across the Sub Saharan region and Africa as a whole.

---

[66] Article 1, African Charter on Human and Peoples' Rights

About half the population of West Africa lives in Nigeria. The West African region has been plagued by wars and conflict in some of its countries. Nigeria and to a lesser extent Cameroon and Niger have been targeted by the Boko Haram terrorist insurgency for a few years now. So the security challenges in the region are formidable.

It is best practice that for Nigeria and the sub region to achieve its development, security and modernization goals, the police must not only provide safety and security for the citizens, but also uphold and promote their constitutional rights. As previously noted, this reality has led to efforts over the past decade by multinational agencies to construct frameworks for policing that encourages effectiveness and promotes constitutional rights-based approach to policing.

At a conference in 2010, the EU and Interpol held a conference to deal with the *challenges of multinational cooperation in policing in*

West Africa.[67] Their goal was to highlight ongoing initiatives in the region and produce proposals that will enhance cooperation in policing in West Africa. It was noted that *'the current EU internal security strategy framework recognised interdependence in Europe's internal and external security'.*[68] It was saliently noted as well that any joint security proposition should be based in policing that embraces and uphold the constitutional rights of citizens.

Many of the challenges previously listed as confronting the Nigerian police are common to practically all countries in the region. Ability to reform policing in Nigeria therefore may require a regional cooperative element and enforcements of African and ECOWAS applicable citizen's charters.

Because of the huge commonalities in the

---

[67] Symposium on 'The External Dimension of EU Police Cooperation: Towards a global and integrated international policing in West African countries', Interpol, 30 September 2010

[68] Ibid

challenges facing policing in West African countries, it is felt a quick overview of developments in several Sub Saharan countries will be a better approach to creating a contextual basis for Nigeria, than a detailed study of just one or two countries.

Also as the biggest and most prosperous nation in ECOWAS, Nigeria should be leading the way and inspiring the others.

So Nigeria can trail an initiative or policy that does not yet exist in any of its ECOWAS neighbours. The countries in this region comes from two main colonial traditions, France (Francophone countries) and England (Anglophone countries).

Hence, their criminal justice system reflects the different approaches of the French (Inquisitorial) and the English (Adversarial) judicial cultures.

POLICE IN FRANCOPHONE WEST AFRICA[69]

As opposed to British West African states, French colonies (Francophone nations) rely more on civil law and many till date continue to apply French Law. Added to the inquisitorial justice system, Francophone nations usually have multiple agencies with a police related functions:

- The gendarmerie.
- The national guard
- The national police,

It is instructive that all the countries of the Sub Saharan region (either Anglophone or Francophone) share the same problems of culture of impunity, lack of independent complaint system, political interference, poor training and working conditions and inadequate funding of the police, all of which are found on the list of the challenges facing Nigerian police stated in Chapter 1.

---

[69] Symposium on 'The External Dimension of EU Police Cooperation: Towards a global and integrated international policing in West African countries', Interpol, 30 September 2010

Burkina Faso[70]

Over the past decade, the country has embarked on a range of reform initiatives within its police operations. With many Burkina distrusting the police as with other countries in the region, the authorities have started to address many of the concerns of its citizens.

In 2003 a new security initiative was introduced, with a focus on crime prevention. In 2005, community policing was introduced and led to the creating of a municipal police force, part of whose remit is to receive complaints from the citizens on police conduct.

In an attempt to broaden the range of recruits in its rank, the police in this country opened its recruitments to civilians from all walks of life. In recent times, the conditions of detention in police formations across the country has been prioritised. Challenges still exist, but there are visible changes observable in Burkina Faso

---

[70] ibid

police compared to a decade ago.[71]

Senegal[72]

Senegal has seen an increase in public interactions with the police over the past few years as its many previous reform initiatives began to bear fruit. Starting with the 1981 reform to integrate women into the police, to its legal reforms in 1999 to the detention rules requiring mandatory access to lawyers and doctors, to its introduction of community policing in the year 2000.

Training was also improved with the introduction of training in constitutional rights and ethical policing being introduced in their police training colleges.

Better protection of minors in detention was later introduced, while its police statutes was redrafted in 2009, which included an obligation to engage with the public and the

---

[71] ibid
[72] ibid

development of a new complaint system.

Ivory Coast[73]

The recent political crisis in this country has made the reputation of the police one of the worst in the region. Police are seen as culprits of constitutional protection violation, including illegal detention, torture, suppression of demonstration and rampant corruption. Impunity has increased and complaints mechanism almost non-existent. As the country begins to rebuild from its years of conflict, reform of the police is gradually rising to the top of the agenda of the government.[74]

Niger[75]

The police in Niger is dominated cripplingly by colonial practices. They suffer from very low numbers and poor infrastructure provision. With its long history of being a political tool by the government, the police

---

[73] ibid
[74] ibid
[75] ibid

suffer from poor image and lack of professionalism. In 2004 and later in 2010, new legislation provided an independent operational platform for the police.

This included structural reforms, including changes to training and recruitment procedures. Special units were also created such as the public order units, but attempts are being made to focus in-service training of officers on protection of constitutional rights of citizens.

With its heavy colonial paradigm and approach to policing, the Niger police still has a long way to go in winning trust of the people and be seen as an independent professional organisation.

Benin[76]

For a long time, police in Benin was highly militarised. In was not until 1991 that the

---

[76] ibid

police were separated from the army, but the public perception has remained largely the same. Suspicion of the police and lack of trust in them is common among the citizenry.

With poor community relations the police find cooperation from the communities virtually non-existent as the people believe them to be corrupt and involved in criminal activities. The trust in government's ability or willingness to reform the police is also weak, especially since the government have refused to implement many of the recommendations of a 2003 report of the state of the police.[77]

POLICE IN ANGLOPHONE WEST AFRICA[78]

With their colonial heritage from the British, all the Anglophone nations face similar challenges as that of their Francophone neighbours. Despite the differences in the judicial heritage and culture, there seem to be distinctively common African elements and

---

[77] ibid
[78] ibid

challenges to policing in the sub Saharan region. This is why an ECOWAS regional cooperative approach may be crucial to success in individual nations.

Sierra Leone[79]

This country has been involved in violent conflict in recent years. As such, the police as with many government institutions ceased to function for many years. With emergency rule commonplace, violence was common tool used by the police. Since the end of hostilities, the poor trust and perception of the police has not changed much, despite some attempts at reform.

With the introduction of community policing, new oversight and control systems established the police reputation of corruption persists, and they are still seen as ruthless and violent. This has not been helped by the police being susceptible to political control and reported recruitment of people of known

---

[79] ibid

criminal background.

Liberia[80]

Like Sierra Leone, Liberia has also had a long civil conflict and period of political instability. The police were seen as agents of the state for the repression of the people during those years and its image is yet to fully recover, even though there has been repeated efforts at reform by the recent democratic governments.

The 2003 post war agreement gives the basis for the transformation agenda of the police in its post-conflict era.

Many of the officers who had committed constitutional rights violations were sacked and new recruitment criteria was developed with focus on professionalization of the police service. About 20% of its officers are now women, thousands of new officers have been

---

[80] ibid

trained in the post conflict period[81].

As with other states in the region, the Liberian police also in 2005 started a community policing initiative with the aim of improving transparency and trust in the police. There has been improvement in the perception of the police but there is still a long way to go before operational excellence can reach a critical mass to substantially elevate public opinion.

Ghana[82]

The oversight and funding are generally perceived to be inadequate in the Ghanaian police service. Several attempts have been made to improve public perception of the police.

A new pay scale was introduced few years

---

81 Symposium on 'The External Dimension of EU Police Cooperation: Towards a global and integrated international policing in West African countries', Interpol, 30 September 2010
[82] ibid

ago for the police officers in Ghana that has improved pay and conditions.

As with other nations in the region, community policing was introduced, but public perception of police as corrupt and lacking in capacity still persist. New efforts are now being made by the government to modernise and better equip the police in this country.

KEY LESSONS FOR NIGERIA

There appears to be a common theme to the state of policing in Sub Saharan Africa. The key headlines are:

- Bad colonial legacy
- Militarisation of the police
- Excessive use of force and brutality
- Impunity
- Lack of trust by the citizens. Many do not see police as being on their side.
- Extra judicial activities
- Poor training and understanding of the law
- Effects of Civil war and conflict

detrimental to constitutionally fair policing
- Corruption
- Inadequate number of officers

All the above key headline agrees with the findings of this research on the Nigerian police based on respondents as explained in Chapter 1. So it would seem that a regional transformation could emerge from solutions posited for Nigeria.

Key lessons for Nigeria based on the regional lessons are as follows:

1. *NAME CHANGE*: Constitutional Change of the Name from Nigeria police Force to Nigeria Police Service. The word "Force" seem to reinforce the militarised nature of policing and getting rid of the word will also help create a better distinction between the police Service and the Military forces.
2. *BETTER INVESTMENT:* The funding

for the police should increase substantially to enable them to develop capability in Intelligence gathering and Forensic Science as well as other protective equipment.

3. *EFFECTIVE AND FAST TRACK DISCIPLINARY and COMPLAINTS SYSTEM:* The culture of impunity that is common in policing is due to lack of effective disciplinary process and a judicial system that can take up to ten years for a case to reach judgment. These have made citizens to lose trust in the police and the judicial system at large. Even in the exceptional cases that a judgement is given against the police after years of litigation, (if they don't simply ignore it), they merely appeal the judgement and that can start another ten year cycle up to the Supreme Court. By that time, the complainant would have either died or no longer interested in the case.

The Nigerian judicial system is very

slow. In a decided case recently an intellectual property infringement case was decided in November 2015, thirty years after the case was filed.[83] There should also be a culture of suspending officers accused of serious breaches pending the determination of their cases. This will act as some disincentive since the officer will not be able to continue working for the length of the case.

4. *BETTER QUALITY OF TRAINING:* It was only in the last three years that the Nigerian Police Academy was upgraded to a degree awarding body. With that will come better trained officers, but this will take a long time to feed into the workforce of the police.

5. *CREATION OF WHISTLE BLOWING LEGISLATION:* As with many organisations in Nigeria, there will be

---

[83] This was the case of a Musician, King Sunny Ade as reported in < http://www.africamusiclaw.com/sunny-ade-wins-n500m-copyright-infringement-lawsuit/> accessed on 13 November 2015.

the good and the bad in the police. The good tend to either keep silent for fear of reprisals or join the bad ones to fit in. An effective independent whistle blowing system will encourage officers to report bad behaviour amongst themselves for the good of the nation.

All the above will be captured in Chapter Six of this book when focus will be on the recommendations to support good governance.

Chapter FOUR

FUNDING CHALLENGES FACING THE NIGERIA POLICE

Funding allocation to the Nigeria police is difficult to fully capture due to the way the nation is organised and a culture of secrecy. Aside from the central funding allocation from the federal budget (for which there are some visibility), there is a web of funding from the various "security budgets" of the federal government as well as that of each of the thirty-six states and Abuja. And by practice, these security budgets are never audited or even disclosed.

There is also occasional private sector funded initiatives and policing projects the value of which are never disclosed. The Governors (as relating to States security budget) have full discretion on how this budget is spent and he/she is answerable to nobody.

All the governors and deputies spoken to by this researcher admit they prefer the status quo secret nature of the security budget. Their overwhelming view is that the secrecy is needed in order not to inform criminals and terrorists of the financial capacity of the state to fight crime. This study finds this sentiment expressed by the governors as self serving and pretentious.

Although the alleged amount of the security allocation to each state can be found, these numbers tend not be denied or confirmed by the states and there is complete mystery about how they are expended and disbursed.

The security allocations are supposed to be used for the security needs of each state, hence why it is shrouded in secrecy, claims all the governors spoken to. This therefore means any allocation to policing by a governor is not financially visible and impossible to quantify, let alone audit.

So any reference to funding of the police in this research will be based largely on some of the disclosed federal budgetary allocation to the police as reported in the media and government sources.

There are many historical factors that created the current perfect storm of crisis in the funding of police in Nigeria. Some will be looked at in the next Chapter, but it will be fair to say that what exists in Nigeria today is what I call *"Policing by Donation"*. The police are able to function at all only through the goodwill of corporate donors, wealthy individuals and community efforts and some state governments. Some recent developments are worthy of mention at this point.

In 1999, the number of police officers in

Nigeria stood at about 118,000 officers approximately. That number had barely changed in the preceding five years due to the refusal of the Abacha military government to recruit new police officers.

So after so many pressure, President Obasanjo, agreed to the recruitment of 40,000 police officers each year for five years. That led to the recruitment of 200,000 new officers, thus tripling the official numbers of serving police officer to about 318,000.

While this was a welcomed development, it also created a crisis of funding as the federal government did not increase the police recurrent budget to match a three-fold increase in overhead cost.

The funding of the police has not recovered from this development ever since. Additionally, the habit of 'envelop funding' by the government where approved funds are released in batches rather than in one swoop has made a bad situation worse. This has led to funds still yet to be released even at the end of the fiscal year. But this will be examined a bit more shortly in this Chapter.

The first observation about the budgetary allocation to the police is that it is a top-down approach rather than bottom up. This means the police headquarters bids for funds in negotiations with the Presidency without any consultation with its local stations of there financial requirements.

So the local police station gets whatever the headquarters can provide, whether that meets its need or not. This realism encourages many local commanders to go into extortion and corrupt practices to make money, not just for personal gains, but also to run their police stations.

Salaries of serving officers seem to be the only certainty for funding (even this is not fully catered for) as all other needs of the local police stations and posts are rarely fully catered for adequately from official funds.[84] From the money needed to feed suspects detained by the police to the cost of fuelling and repairing operational vehicles of the police, these are all left to the local commanders to source.

This reality is a major justification many commanders use to justify their foray into corrupt practices and bribe collection.

For instance, in 2015, N5.9Billion was budgeted for the Overhead Cost for police commands across the country, but the Inspector General of police (IGP) at the time Suleiman Abba went to the media to announce that that entire allocation cannot buy fuel to operate all police vehicles for a three-month period, much less the whole year and other operational needs it was supposed to cover.

---

[84] <http://saharareporters.com/2011/11/07/conditions-nigerias-police-force-0> accessed on 5 January 2016

So the question is where do local commanders get the funds to operate police vehicles for the rest of the year? The answer is too commonly accepted as corruption and bribery.

As reported by Vanguard Newspaper[85] in February 2015, the IGP lamented as follows:

> "..paucity of funds occasioned by the envelope concept of budgeting have become an impediment towards police meeting up with its constitutional requirements. Every year the police were given specific amounts for its Capital and Recurrent budgets tagged ceiling or envelope that never reflected the enormous size, scope and responsibility and actual needs of the force".[86]

---

[85] <http://www.vanguardngr.com/2015/02/2015-budget-n5-9bn-cant-fuel-police-vehicles-in-3-months-igp/,> accessed on 6 January 2016
[86] ibid

To evidence his claim, the IGP stated further to the media that:

> "... in 2014 budget, a capital vote of N218 billion was proposed but it was later replaced with an envelope of N7.34 billion, adding that even out of that, only N3,453,492,502 representing 47 per cent was released as at December 31 of the year. He also confirmed that out of N8,499,861,314 that was appropriated for Overhead cost expenditure for 2014, only N5,708,229,318 was released and out of that, N5,000,000 was deducted at source for electricity bills, while the sum of N2,791,631,996 representing 32 percent was not released."[87]

In 2015, the overhead budgetary allocation to the police was N8.4Billion,[88] but as noted by the IGP at the time, though this allocation was inadequate, the police will still not be given the

---

[87] ibid
[88] ibid

total allocated sum as several deductions are made from source for all manner of reasons.

In the 2016 Budget proposals,[89] the allocations to the police related areas are still in flux as the budget has not yet been passed by the National Assembly.

Media reports[90] show that the trend in police funding is downward over the past few years. But there is also the curious habit of allocated funds not being fully released to the Nigeria police by the government.

It is anyone's guess what actually happens to these shortfalls in allocated funds. In late 2015, the IGP, Solomon Arase again took to the media to lament budgetary challenges

---

[89] Wale Odunsi, '2016 Budget: Breakdown Of Sums Allocated To Presidency, Mdas, Others - Dailypost Nigeria' (DailyPost Nigeria, 2015) <http://dailypost.ng/2015/12/26/2016-budget-breakdown-of-sums-allocated-to-presidency-mdas-others/> accessed 5 January 2016.
[90] 'Latest News • DAAR Group • DAAR Communications' (DAAR Communications, 2016) <http://www.daargroup.com/daar-group/latest-news/vanguardngr-poor-budgetary-allocation-stalls-police-recruitment-minister-2,> accessed 11 January 2016.

facing the police.

In a media interview, Arase further stated:

- "In the year 2010, the police asked for over N45 billion in the overhead budget, but was given a paltry N16 billion that was hardly able to take care of stationery.
- In the same year, the police asked for over N53 billion under the capital budget, but was given about N39 billion"[91].

Further he expressed regret that "the N57 billion appropriated for the police in the 2010 to 2014 budgets are outstanding but has not been released till date"[92].

As evidenced above, the budgetary announcement and budgetary allocation in reality are not the same in Nigeria. An amount

---

[91] (2016) <http://newtelegraphonline.com/poor-funding-responsible-for-corruption-in-police-ig> accessed 11 January 2016.

[92] ibid

is announced as budgeted, but the police never get that amount in reality. If deductions are not made from source at the whim of the politicians, parts of budgets are withheld sometimes for years as evidenced by IGP Arase above.

Detailed analysis show that there is no logic or discernable pattern to the federal funding allocation to the Nigeria police. The sums are haphazard and always substantially less than the amount requested by the police every year.

From all indications and analysis, the Nigeria police get funding from FIVE main sources:

1. *Federal Allocation by the Federal Government.* This is the only funding that some figures are available for. This is the only constitutionally certain funding source for the police as a federal institution. All other sources are discretionary, uncertain and at time whimsical.

2. *Funding and support for each state command by the state Governors from their state security budgets.* This amount is never published, hence it is shrouded in secrecy.

3. *Private sector contributions.* Again no figure exists nationally for this. Occasionally private sector organisation as part their Corporate Social Responsibility obligations make contributions either financially or materially to the police.

4. *International funding from bi and multilateral institutions.* There are some funding from global organisations of specific areas of policing. This can be in form of sponsorship of events to training and equipment supply.

5. *Local communities contributions.* Communities sometimes make contributions to the police to support local patrols, police post and community security. Again there is no

central figure compiled nationally for this.

Given the lack of data for items 2 to 5 above, any analysis of police funding can only be done through analysis of Federal funding as Nigeria has only a federal police service.

All other funding sources identified are optional, irregular and occasional in nature. For example, States in Nigeria do not actually give money to the police. What they do is identify a need and procure that need for the exclusive use of the police for operations in their own state alone.

A typical example the the donation of patrol vehicles to the police by state Governors. The public is never told how much these vehicles cost, but the Governors simply announce the donation to the media.

A recent case is that of Lagos state that donated vehicles and an helicopter (photos below) to the Nigerian police but only for use in Lagos state[93]. As customary, the governor did not announce exactly how much these donations cost.

Source: Vanguard Newspaper published on 27 November 2015

---

[93] 'Photos: Ambode Presents Helicopters, Gunboats, Vehicles To Police' (Vanguard News, 2015) <http://www.vanguardngr.com/2015/11/photos-ambode-presents-helicopters-gunboats-vehicles-to-police/> accessed 11 January 2016.

Source: Vanguard Newspaper published on 27 November 2015

Source: Vanguard Newspaper published on 27 November 2015

The side effect of these state level additional funding sources is that the capacity and capability of the Nigeria police now vary substantially from state to state. The main argument for the sustenance of a federal police structure is equality of standards regardless of your state.

But because of the poor funding of the police federally, many state governors have stepped in to support the police in their respective states, thus creating a two tier police force.

The richer states like Lagos donate essential equipment to the police for operations in their state, but poor states do not, thus rely more on the federal funding only. This could have some displacement effect on crime as criminals migrate away from better patrolled states to poorly patrolled ones.

A single source of data on federal allocations to the police has proven difficult during this research. Repeated enquiries to the main NGOs and the Nigerian police did not yield any response.

As with much information provided by the police authorities, only a detailed search of the print media yielded some results.

The current Inspector General of Police (IGP) Solomon Arase in an interview with the Daily Trust newspaper as reported by the African Defence publication on 24 December 2015, lamented the budgetary challenges facing the police.

In this interview, IGP Arase stated that the gaps between what **recurrent funds** police requests and how much is allocated is massive. His figures are captured by the following table.

FINANCIAL YEAR	WHAT WAS REQUESTED BY POLICE (N)	WHAT WAS APPROVED and ALLOCATED (N)
2013	N56Billion	N7Billion

FINANCIAL YEAR	WHAT WAS REQUESTED BY POLICE (N)	WHAT WAS APPROVED and ALLOCATED (N)
2014	N45Billion	N16Billion
2015	N71Billion	N5Billion

Figure 10 : Police financial requests versus allocation[94]

According to Arase, these multi-year shortfalls affected equally capital funding of the police as it affects the recurrent allocations. Arase stated that this have led to failures of many police capital projects and the police now left with a cumulative active liability profile of N54bn as at 2015[95].

---

[94] 'The Nigerian Police Force Is So Broke, It Can Barely Afford Stationery, Says IGP Arase - The Scoopng' (The ScoopNG, 2015) <http://www.thescoopng.com/nigerian-police-force-broke-can-barely-afford-stationery/> accessed 11 March 2016.
[95] Jeff McKaughan, 'Nigerian National Police Budget Too Small - African Defense' (African Defense, 2015) <http://www.african-defense.com/defense-news/nigerian-

The effects of these scarcity of funds to the police has created operational and reputational problems for the force. Operationally, many police divisional officers do not have the funds to manage the operations of their division.

Money to fuel and repair official vehicles has to be found somehow. Most people detained by police who are supposed to be fed by the police while in custody have to send messages to their relative to bring food for them.

This is due to lack of funding for their feeding. The state of many police station is unsightly and an embarrassment to many serving officers, with many operating out of dilapidated shacks and porta cabins.

Reputation-wise, many police officers resort to bribe collection, extortion and other corrupt

national-police-budget-too-small/> accessed 15 January 2016.

practices to be able to raise funds to pay for what official funding should have paid for.

A divisional police officer interviewed gave an example of three new officers who were transferred to his division from another state, having to sleep in the police station for the first four months of their posting due to non payment of transfer and relocation allowances by the police authorities.

According to him, these officers had to resort to bribe collection to raise money for their accommodation.

The inadequate funding of the police manifests itself in many ways and can be seen in the following areas:

a) Poor Level of Pay and Conditions

b) Inadequate number of serving police personnel

c) Inadequate Operational Equipment, (Vehicles, Office Equipment, etc).

d) Poor Arms and Ammunition

e) Poor Forensic Laboratory

f) Poor Quality and Inadequate Data Bank

g) Poor Level of Intelligence Gathering and Facilities

Many serving and retired officers interviewed for this research indicated their dislike for the top heavy budgetary implementation by the police. It was claimed by many officers interviewed that about 70% of recurrent and capital expenditure decisions is taken at the highest level from the Police Headquarters.

This leaves an already top down budget implemented in a top down way. This is why many at the State command levels complain of starvation of funds from the headquarters. They just do not see the funds promised as the Headquarters would have mopped up most of the funds available with many being lost to top level corruption.

This has left many state commands starved of

essential funding. This is why the states that can afford it, help the police in their states with additional supplies and donations. But this is not a given that they will provide this support and many Governors use such donations to buy influence and loyalty of the state police commissioners.

This research also found that basic working tools were not available to many police commands. Ninety per cent of officers interviewed admit to not having access to basic stationery to work in the police station. Seventy percent had to buy their own shoes as replacements are rarely provided. This is a prevailing picture nationwide.

CANNIBALIZATION AND DUPLICATION OF POLICING EFFORT

As noted earlier, there are several organizations that have been established to do policing functions in Nigeria. These organisations consume billions of naira that would have been allocated to the police. They also create inefficiencies in back office activities as they duplicate all the support departments that already exist within the police.

To add to the cannibalization of the main police, the Special Branch, (SB) was expunged in mid 1970s from the police force but rebranded the National Security Organisation (NSO). The NSO was later changed into the Criminal Intelligence Bureau (CIB), which later transformed into today's State Security Service (SSS).

So despite the Constitutional provision that there shall be only one police service in Nigeria, the following agencies have been established to do policing related duties, by either taking over partially or completely duties of the police:

1) The Economic and Financial Crimes Commission (EFCC)
2) Federal Roads Safety Commission (FRSC)

3) Independent Corrupt Practices Commission (ICPC)
4) Nigerian Security and Civil Defence Corps (NSCDC)
5) The State Security Service (SSS)
6) The Code of Conduct Bureau (CCB)
7) Code of Conduct Tribunal (CCT)
8) The Vehicle Inspection Organisation (VIO)
9) National Drug Law Enforcement Agency (NDLEA)

To evidence the claim in this study of these multiple agencies taking away valuable money needed for core policing, it is necessary to analyse a typical year financial allocation to some of these agencies. So 2014 will be our sample year.

In that year the budgetary allocations to some of the key policing agencies outside the core police force were as follows:

	RECURRENT BUDGET (N)	CAPITAL BUDGET (N)	TOTAL BUDGET ALLOCATION (N)
ICPC	4,542,989,874	132,897,643	4,675,887,517
CCB	1,856,158,560	1,006,147,091	2,862,305,651
CCT	460,229,424	52,440,642	512,670,066
EFCC	8,838,694,493	1,406,674,677	10,245,369,170
AGENCIES TOTAL	**15,698,072,351**	**2,598,160,053**	**18,296,232,404**

Figure 11: Budgets of some agencies with policing related duties[96]

From the above table, just four of these parallel agencies performing policing related functions (but there are more than four of them in existence) were allocated just over **N18Billion.**

In that year the combined allocation to the

---

[96] CLEEN Foundation Policy brief analysis of 2014 Appropriation Bill for Anticorruption Agencies

core operations of the Nigerian Police Force was about **N23Billion**. So merging these four agencies alone could instantly double the budget available to the police. There are a few other agencies in addition to these four. These were itemized earlier in this research.

SHORTAGE OF OPERATIONAL FUNDS

The fact is the budget of the police is 'voodoo economics'. The headquarters seem to just make up numbers based on its own priorities, knowing that 70% of the funds will be managed by the headquarters.

The needs and requirements of the various commands are not compiled, so the commands make do with whatever it gets, hoping the state governments and other funding sources will bail it out. This is not efficient or sensible.

The financial constraints on the police also affects its ability to kit its laboratories or conduct reasonable intelligence operations on a consistent basis. A senior police source narrated an example of how lack of funds to conduct decent intelligence operations handicaps the police. The source stated that the police was tracking a known drug trafficker with the aim of collecting actionable intelligence that can be used for prosecution.

The suspect lodged himself in a suite at a top hotel in Abuja, Nigeria. The best practice would have been for the police to book the suite next door and listen in on the suspect from there.

But the police command could not find the funds to pay for the suite next door. Hence the police could only listen in and track the suspect while in public places around the hotel.

They gave up after a few days when it became clear that the suspect never discussed anything of interest while in public places. This is just an example of how lack of funds is eroding the capacity of the police to deliver on its legal mandate to protect the public and prosecute criminals.

This research received several examples similar to the foregoing on the failure of the police occasioned by scarcity of funds. A serious analysis reveals how all Inspector Generals of Police in the past decade use the media repeatedly to announce the financial difficulties of the police and begging for more funds. This confirms that the funding shortage of the police is historical in nature.

From its regional formations of four centres in 1960, the Nigeria Police has grown to reflect the expansion of the political and demographic structure of the country. Now there are 36 states plus the Federal Capital City, Abuja. The country now has 774 local government areas, and 37 state command centres.

When a state was created, a start-up grant is usually allocated to assist in setting up infrastructure for the new state. Sadly, the setting up of police was never included in these financial disbursements. Consequently, they operated from temporary accommodation not suitable for policing duties.

The budgetary allocation to the police has not kept pace with its ever enlarging office and operational facilities requirements. With the exception of the Headquarters building, police offices are renowned for being the one of the ugliest and most dilapidated looking in all the states. Some have become hazard to the serving officers, much less the visiting public. The cells are horrible, unhygienic and health risks for detainees.

Many of the police offices visited by this researcher did not have running water and it is a common sight to see police posts being illuminated by candles at night. The table below shows the size and spread of the police office infrastructure nationwide. This list is by no means exhaustive.

No	Level of command	Number in the country
1	Village Posts	5,000
2	Police Stations	5,515
3	Police Divisions	1,115
4	Area Commands	123
5	State Commands plus the Federal Capital	37
6	Zonal Commands	12
7	State CIDs plus FCT	37
8	Force Headquarters	1
9	Force Headquarters Annex	1
10	Police Dog Sections	37
11	Border Patrol Stations	4
12	Railway police Command	7
13	Mounted Training Centres	37
14	Medical Centres	37
15	Central police Band	36
16	Marine Unit HQ	1

Figure 12 : Police fixed location inventory[97]

---

[97] From multiple sources (anonymity protected)

To recap, the funding challenges of the police can be summarized as follows:

1) *Top Down Budgetary Process*

   The budgeting process in the police is top down. The needs of the various commands are not captured in the process. This may be partly due to the fact that the police top officers realize that they will never be given the funding they really need, so no point doing the compilation of needs across the commands. But it is a major problem when funds are disbursed without reference to the needs of each command.

   Each police division serve different population strength and some are busier than others. So the financial need of each will be different. A bottom up process of capturing the needs of all the stations, all the divisions and all the commands plus the need of the headquarters will allow a proportional distribution of the limited allocated budget. This does not happen currently.

2) *Lack of Funding Visibility*

As stated previously, the sources of funding to the police are many. But lots of them are shrouded in secrecy. Even the federally allocated budget is not very clear as there are ad hoc funding for specially projects or events like the national elections. These figures are never clearly announced. So getting a clear visibility of police funding is impossible.

Eighty percent of senior police sources interviewed believe that the top officers in the force seem to like this confusion as it makes it easier for them to steal public funds without clear auditable or accounting checks. It is hardly easy to prove theft of an amount you do not know exists.

Also with total secrecy of how much all the states give to the police from their secret "security Budget", finding out how much is given to the police yearly is impossible in Nigeria. In fact, the size of the states "Security Budget" is a secret. This lack of complete visibility makes it difficult for the police to convincingly argue that they need more funding and exactly how much is needed.

3) *Lack of Strategic Planning and Continuity*

As a society, Nigeria is not good at long term planning. And with the constant change of government that beleaguered the nation for many decades, each new government developed the habit to throwing away all its predecessors plans and projects and started all over again with its own vanity programme. There was no continuity of planning or implementation. This is the same with the police. With the lack of tenure security by the police chiefs, each new one seem to throw away the plans in place and starts his own new plan.

This lack of continuity is problematic. Ninety percent of officers interviewed opined that each new police chief want his or her own opportunity to steal funds, hence the start of his own fresh agenda, rather than continue with that of his predecessor and complete it. This problem also has the effect of ballooning the budgets of major initiatives to an astronomical level.

4) *Serious Corruption at the Headquarter Level*

With seventy percent of allocated budget being controlled by the Headquarters, the conventional wisdom is that most of an already inadequate budget is creamed off by the top officers of the police. This has led to a clear divide between the top brass and the frontline officers. The frontline officers do a lot of complaining while the top brass give a slightly rosier picture of a poor service. While ninety-five percent of junior frontline officers interviewed said they believe their superiors are not honest with management of police funding, only thirty percent of senior officers (Commissioner rank and above) believe this is a problem.

5) *Inadequate Involvement of the Private Sector due to police Reputational problems.*

The police brand is so toxic in Nigeria that many private sector organizations will rather not have anything to do with the police unless they feel they have no choice. This has led to poor financial contribution or support of the police by the organized private sector. This deprives the police of needed additional funds they could otherwise have access to.

6) *Lack of Key Centralised operational departments and loss of Economies of scale.*

In the 70s, there used to be centralized police vehicle workshops nationwide for the repair and maintenance of official vehicles. These have all been closed down.

So each police station goes to different private mechanic workshops to repair and maintain their vehicles all over the country. This loses economies of scale and increases the cost to the police. The consequence is both a high repair and maintenance cost to the police and a pervasive culture of badly maintained vehicles, due to lack of funds.

Seventy percent of police officers interviewed said lack of good operational vehicles hinders their capacity to patrol their cities. This percentage rises to ninety percent for officers outside of Lagos and Abuja. It is therefore evident that the bad state of patrol vehicles hinders police operations daily. It is not uncommon for a police vehicle to break down during a chase.

7) *Reasonable number of officers but poor pay and conditions.*

As explained in the next chapter, the number of officers on the books in Nigeria is not too bad, but their productivity is appalling. So a better paid, better equipped and better supported but smaller police force could be better than the status quo. Such an approach could reduce the overall staffing budget of the police with fewer but more effective officers.

8) *Problem of State focused additional support by Governors.*

With the exception of a few financially buoyant states, most states in Nigeria are not financially viable, poor and dependent on federal grants to survive.

As illustrated earlier in this Chapter a state like Lagos is very rich and has the means to provide additional support to the police in vehicles and other essential infrastructure. But by convention, these support can only be used for policing in Lagos and not another state.

This creates a situation where a few states have better equipment (as a result of additional support from the Governors) while others are so deprived they cannot conduct any major criminal operation. If the support provided by the states are allowed to be used across other states, this could help support the police over a bigger command area. This spirit of reciprocity and cooperation does not exist currently in Nigeria.

9) *Reputational Hindrances to Effective Community support for the police.*
   As with organized private sector,

communities have the same distrust of the police due to the bad reputation the force has in the communities. So there is lack of cooperation and support for the police by many citizens in the communities. This fact deprives the police of additional support that communities could provide if better engaged.

10) *Lack of culture of Respect and Appreciation of the police*

In many countries, the police, just like the armed forces, are treated with such respect and appreciation that they enjoy many discounts and free offerings from the general public. With free travel on public transport, discounts at shops and hotels to special offers just for being in the police. These "benefits" are voluntarily provided by the population in support of the men and women who puts their lives on the line for the benefit of society. None of these takes place in

Nigeria.

The police have such a bad reputation nobody wants to have anything to do with them. If these wider benefits exist, the police authorities will save lots of money, thus making their limited budget go further. But in Nigeria, the police budget has to be used to pay for their transport etc all over the country. These are funds that could be saved if the wider society embraces the police and offer them needed appreciation.

11) *Lack of Financial Accountability.*
It is not uncommon to read of millions of naira being allocated for various projects by the police authorities and yet the outcome expected is not delivered and the funds have disappeared. There is no accountability by the police authorities for the funds allocated to them. Ninety percent of police officers interviewed stated that they believe the police force

is not financially accountable. This supports the trend in this research of police officers being honest and self aware in ways that aligns their perception with that of the general public.

The only other official body (outside those intimately connected with the day to day policing itself) that can draw attention to the maladministration in the police is the Senate Committee on Police Affairs. But they do not have any direct power other than legislative changes and their access to the court of public opinion.

But they are known for making some noise, but then keep quite soon after. Examples of the corruption problem abound in the media. In a media report BribeNigeria.com quoting Leadership newspaper wrote in its editorial that:

"No less than N2.046 billion has been

budgeted for the upgrade of facilities at the various police colleges across the country, yet the condition of living in the colleges remains pitiable[98]".

The police authorities could not account for what happened to the allocated funds even though the allocated funds have been spent with no commensurate outcome. This is typical in Nigeria. Such funds are managed by the headquarters who are considered corrupt even by frontline serving police officers. It is not uncommon for the police authorities to shift blame of non performance to the other supervising police agencies such as the Ministry of Police Affairs and the Police Service Commission.

---

[98] 'Nigeria: Investigation – N2.04 Billion Budgeted For Police Colleges In Four Years | Bribenigeria.Com' (Bribenigeria.com, 2016) <http://www.bribenigeria.com/nigeria-investigation-n2-04-billion-budgeted-for-police-colleges-in-four-years/> accessed 11 January 2016.

While the police complain of lack of adequate funding, they are not properly accounting for the funds being disbursed to them currently. And there has never been any meaningful probe or penalty for this failure.

12) *Funding shortage had led to lack of universal Supply of Basic tools for frontline officers.*

The Nigerian police lack many basic tools of the trade for policing as a result of the budgetary constraints. For instance, supply of body armour is virtually non existent for frontline officers. Only five percent of police officers interviewed stated that they have been issued with any protective kit whatsoever. As a result of this, there is an over reliance on offensive policing by officers. Knowing they have no protection from attack, there is danger that many officer will shoot first and ask questions later. One of the old police training booklet shown to this researcher lists some of the basic equipment an officer on the beat should have.

This booklet stated that to to perform efficiently, a Constable on frontline duty should be equipped with the following basic kits: -

a) Uniform
b) Rain coats
c) Note book
d) Official shoes
e) Sweaters for use in cold parts of Nigeria
f) Radio
g) Torch lights
h) Batons

No single officer interviewed confirmed they have been issued with all of the foregoing. And this is not an exhaustive list. Yet fifty percent of the officers confirmed they have been issued with firearms. It is a sad case of you cannot have a rain coat but you can have a gun.

The financial shortage facing the police has led to many officers to seek short cuts in the course of their duty. This also has exacerbated the already poor reputation and regard for the police amongst the population.

Giving AK47 or any other gun for that matter to an officer who is poorly paid, poorly equipped, lowly regarded and non appreciation from the population, and sending him into the hostile crime infested streets of Nigeria inner cities is asking for trouble.

This along with poor training tends to make officers unduly aggressive and oppressive to the citizens they are supposed to protect. With civil conflicts in the recent past in multiple countries in the West African sub region, Nigerian criminals have been able to source cheap sophisticated and modern firearms to perpetrate their illegal trade in death and violence.

The sad reality is that many criminals are better equipped than the police. The standard issue to the frontline Nigerian police is still the historical AK47. There are weekly reports of police officers running away from armed robbery locations partly due to the superior guns the criminals display.[99]

A major consequence of the poor funding of the police is the inadequate training regime or opportunities for serving officers. Each state command had a Deputy Commissioner of Police (DCP) in charge of training.

But they tend not to have any team or budget to work with. The opportunities for capacity building through training is poor supply. Many

---

[99] Some of the many cases reported in the media are listed below: (All accessed on 15 January 2016)
a). <https://www.naij.com/348185-armed-robbers-stormed-access-bank-in-agbor-police-fled.html>
b). <http://www.tori.ng/news/18866/drama-as-policemen-run-away-after-robbers-shoot-ma.html>
c). <http://www.nairaland.com/2878636/policemen-abscond-robbers-shoot-guard/1>

officers who want to do better are constrained by a system that does not value training and hence does not fund it.

This lack of training opportunities also have operational implications with paucity of funds making firearms training dangerously inadequate. Officers do not receive any routine or ongoing firearms training and certification after the initial training received when joining the force.

It is not uncommon to meet officers who have been in the police for fifteen years and have received no firearms training for the entire fifteen years. This is one of the contributory factors to the many cases of accidental discharges of firearms by officers that are reported from time to time.

The funding crisis facing the police has affected all areas of its operation in negative ways. Like previously stated, without the donations of other bodies and institutions, the police in Nigeria will not be able to survive for more than a few months on its annual budgetary allocations.

Chapter FIVE

CHALLENGES OF PERSONNEL EDUCATION AND TRAINING FACING THE NIGERIA POLICE

Public confidence in the police is at an all time low as shown in the research findings in Chapter One. As noted in figure two, one hundred percent of the public responded that they have no confidence in the police. Even eighty percent of police officers questioned agree with the public.

On crime prevention, again one hundred percent of the public responded that they are dissatisfied with the performance of the police. Interestingly ninety-five per cent of police officers said they are equally dissatisfied with their organisation's performance. Many said they believe they can do better with better training and tools to do the job. In this chapter, the challenges of training and recruitment will be examined.

To fully understand the challenges the police face with regards to its personnel, it will be necessary to examine the following:

1) The number of serving officers per head of population.

2) The number of officers actually available for front line police work compared with the total number on the books as available.

3) The recruitment practices and standards of the police.

4) The training regime of new recruits.

5) The continuous professional development of serving officers.

6) Effect of the slicing off of traditional police functions into multiple enforcement agencies outside the command and control of the Nigeria Police Force.

1. THE NUMBERS OF SERVING OFFICERS PER HEAD OF POPULATION.

Initial searches could not find credible information within the ECOWAS region on comparative numbers of police officers per head of population. Even within Nigeria, credible figures on current police officers that could be found were a few years old already. On the Police Service Commission (PSC) website, the most up to date annual report available is for 2011.[100]

So, further analysis had to be done at the United Nations to obtain some numbers based on the periodic research and data requests of the European Institute for Crime

---

[100] http://www.psc.gov.ng/annual-reports.html, Accessed on 26th November 2015

Prevention and Control Affiliated with the United Nations (HEUNI). The International Statistics on Crime and Justice[101] interprets police numbers as that of the frontline officers only, excluding back-office support personnel and other staff.

In its 2010 report on its questionnaire to participating countries, HEUNI[102] advised that, *"The 10th United Nations Global Counter-Terrorism Strategy (UNGCTS) questionnaire defines "police personnel or law enforcement personnel" as **"personnel in public agencies whose principal functions are the prevention, detection and investigation of crime and the apprehension of alleged offenders.***

Data concerning support staff (secretaries, clerks, etc.) should be excluded from your replies." This approach will be employed in

---

[101] European Institute for Crime Prevention and Control Affiliated with the United Nations (HEUNI) Publication Series (2010 and 2013)
[102] ibid

this book as well. As already identified in the introduction to this research paper, there is a serious challenge with obtaining up to date data on many areas.

As a regional context, Africa as a whole, has a lower number of police personnel per 100,000 populations of all regions in the world. In fact in its 2010 and 2013 survey, HEUNI found Africa to have the lowest median numbers of personnel per 100,000 of population.[103] It is against this lowest regional base that Nigeria feature.

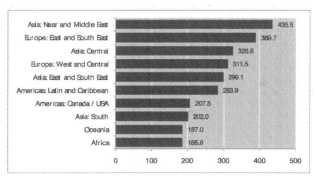

Figure 13: Police per 1000 population by regions and sub regions (median)[104]

---

[103] ibid
[104] ibid

In its report on police numbers within the United Nations members, HEUNI found that

> "Absolute police personnel figures are quite clearly dependent on the population size (corr. 0.93). police personnel rates per 100,000 population vary significantly between countries. The median is 303.3, the mean 341.8, the standard deviation 241.5. The distribution is positively skewed. Results imply that there is a minimum number of police officers per 100,000 population that is necessary in any country. Only four countries worldwide show police personnel values lower than 100 officers per 100,000 population".[105]

Nigeria is not one of the four countries noted as exception. This will suggest that based on sheer numbers of active police officers per head of population, Nigeria is not doing too badly.

---

[105] ibid

In its most up to date Annual Report,[106] the PSC, claimed in 2011 the total establishment numbers (Numbers that are supposed to be employed) was 508,770 police officers. But only 330,480 officers were in post.

However, in its 2013 updated data, the United Nations ranks Nigeria[107] as 6th in the world in terms of sheer number of police officers, (see the table below).

Based on its data, the United Nations states that the *global standard for police numbers per 100,000 population is about 340.* UN then advised on a minimum of 220 per 100,000 people[108].This 220 is considered the average for minimum effective policing.

---

[106] PCS 2011 Annual Report <
http://www.psc.gov.ng/files/2011-Annual-Report.pdf>
accessed 10 November 2015
[107] 'United Nations Office On Drugs And Crime' (Unodc.org, 2016)
<https://www.unodc.org/unodc/index.html?ref=menutop>
accessed 11 November 2015.
[108] ibid

What this number does not factor-in however is the difference between the number of serving officers on the books and the actually number available for frontline policing duties. In the case of Nigeria this will be a major consideration as will be demonstrated later, as many as up to 40% of service police officers are not available for public policing duties due to private security duties they have been assigned with VIPs and government officials.

WORLD RANKING (By police Numbers)	COUNTRY	POLICE NUMBERS	LATEST RELIABLE FIGURE AVAILABLE (Per 100,000 Population)	YEAR
1	India	1,731,537	138	2013
-	China [109]	1,500,000 (Estimate)	120 (Estimate)	2013
2	Russia	745,607	522	2013

---

[109] China is not included in this data, but estimates put its People's Armed Force at between 660,000 (government reported) and 1.5 million (unofficial) members.

WORLD RANKING (By police Numbers)	COUNTRY	POLICE NUMBERS	LATEST RELIABLE FIGURE AVAILABLE (Per 100,000 Population)	YEAR
3	USA	626,942	196	2013
4	Brazil	536,018	268	2013
5	Mexico	454,126	371	2013
6	**Nigeria**	**360,000**	**207**	**2013**
8	Japan	257,100	202	2013
11	South Africa	194,852	368	2013
14	UK (England and Wales)	127,909	225	2013

Figure 14: Police per 100,000 population by country produced by UN[110] and Media publications[111]

---

[110] ibid
[111] 'South Africa's Police Force Vs The World' (Businesstech.co.za, 2015) <http://businesstech.co.za/news/general/95069/south-

The rankings in Fig. 14 above relates to the sheer numbers of police officers. There is a different ranking result if done by police per 100,000 of population. In this case, the smaller countries have the widest police coverage. For instance, the Vatican City comes as one of the top nations in terms of its police coverage. It is reported that of the 450 people that live in the Vatican, 130 are police officers.

That makes it to have one officer per three citizens. For the record, the UNODC[112] places Macau, a Chinese region as having the highest per capita police force in the world. Macau has 1,087 police officers per 100,000. (It has 6,157 officers and a population of only 566,725).[113] With 360,000 police officers and a police to 100,000 population[114] ratio of 207

---

africas-police-force-vs-the-world/> accessed 11 February 2016.

[112] UN's Office on Drugs and Crime

[113] ibid

[114] This is based on the official population of Nigeria based on the last census. There is widespread believe that the nation's population has far outgrown the official figures. A new census is due in 2016.

(in 2013), at first glance it would seem Nigeria is reasonably resourced in terms of police numbers. The PSC report in 2011 stated that there are over 100,000 vacancies within the police.

This high water mark of numbers of serving officers was partly due to a Presidential Directive in 2006 by President Obasanjo that 50,000 officers should be recruited.[115]

There was an earlier Presidential instruction to recruit 40,000 personnel annually between the years 2001 and 2004, but this was not implementable according to a very senior police source interviewed, because all the police training institutions could only accommodate 14,000 intakes per annum.

No provision was made for expansion of these training capacity. This is typical of Nigeria it

---

[115] <http://allafrica.com/stories/200604270229.html> accessed on 9 February 2016

seems where verbal announcements are not followed up by effective resource allocation.

2. THE AMOUNT OF OFFICERS ACTUALLY AVAILABLE FOR FRONT LINE POLICE WORK COMPARED WITH THE TOTAL NUMBER ON THE BOOKS AS AVAILABLE.

The number of police officers on the books do not reflect in frontline policing all over Nigeria. The difficulty and challenge the police face in Nigeria is that not all the serving police officers on the books are available for frontline and public police duties.

Despite a thriving private security industry, most VIPs and wealthy Nigerians as well as most senior public/government officers have police officers attached to them for personal security.

This is an endemic problem for the police institution in Nigeria as the number of officers actually available for frontline policing are a far cry from the number of officers on the payroll. Getting exact figure of officers attached to VIPs and wealthy individuals is impossible in Nigeria as the practice is not documented by the police authorities.

In 2015, there was another announcement of a directive to withdraw police from private citizens, but that was never implemented as with such previous announcements. But real official figures are not available for police on private security duties. The media reported at the time that over 130,000 police officers[116] are deployed to provide security to wealthy Nigerians.

If this figure is to be believed, it means close to forty percent of the police on the payroll unavailable to do public frontline policing duties. So the number of officers actually available for frontline police works makes the nation look under-policed.

---

[116] <http://www.vanguardngr.com/2015/08/withdrawal-of-officers-from-vips-police-deploy-men-to-airports-highways-to-enforce-directive/ > accessed on 29 November 2015

In an interview granted to Sahara Reporters in 2015, a Divisional Police Officer, Hayatu Usman, (a Chief Superintendent ranked officer) moaned as follows:

> "We are handicapped as we have insufficient number of personnel. Almost all the VIPs reside here and 60 to 70 percent of the policemen deployed to their homes on guard duties are from here".[117]

There have been several government announcements that police officers will be withdrawn from providing private security service for the VIPs and wealthy Nigerians, but no visible action of withdrawal has been evident as the culture persists at an epidemic level.

In a 2014 article in Daily Trust newspaper, Eugene Enahoro (a Columnist) complained

---

[117]

<http://saharareporters.tumblr.com/post/12473436292/the-conditions-of-nigerias-police-force> accessed on 29 November 2015.

almost with resignation that: *police authorities constantly defend their poor performance by claiming a shortage of personnel, equipment and operational funds. While undoubtedly true, it's also true that their mobile force is not being utilised to its maximum. There appears to be an over concentration on escorting, protecting and guarding "big men," especially those who hold political office.*[118]

As stated earlier, with 360,000 police officers and a police to 100,000 population ratio of 207 (in 2013), Nigeria appears to be above the United Nations recommended ratio of 200. But if allowance is made for the many officers not actually available for public policing work, then Nigeria ratio will be about 127.

This will make Nigeria clearly under-policed. This reality is the reason for perennial request from the police hierarchy for more officers.

---

[118]

<http://www.dailytrust.com.ng/daily/index.php/opinion/38500 -v-i-p-protection-the-civilised- way#zkG8Xis6SHmsIMWQ.99> accessed on 30 November 2015.

With a substantial percentage of police officers tied down in private security and escorting work for the rich and famous, the police in Nigeria is under-resourced practically speaking although they may look adequate in theoretical terms of the overall number on payroll.

Sixty percent of the general public interviewed do believe Nigeria need more police officers on the frontline, but few are aware of the scale of officers tied to private security duties even though the practice is commonly known.

However, sixty percent of police officers interviewed do not believe officers number is the main challenge.

Rather they believe it is the training and equipment that is inadequate. Especially defensive kits like bullet proof vests for instance.

3. THE RECRUITMENT PRACTICES AND STANDARDS OF THE POLICE.

To join the Nigeria police, there are usually three pathways, as a Recruit Constable, a Cadet Inspector or Cadet ASP.

The Recruit Constable route requires only passes in GCSE 'O' Level School certificate qualification, Credits in GCSE is required for Cadet Inspector, while a Graduate level degree, Advance Level Certificate (from the police academy) or equivalent is required for the Cadet ASP route.

As noted on its website, the CLEEN Foundation referenced the report of the Presidential Committee on Police Reforms titled *"Motion without Movement"* that currently, recruitment into the Nigeria police Force is based on the following qualifications.[119]

a. Age:[120]

- Recruit Constable: Not less than 17 or more than 25 years
- Cadet Inspector: Not less than 19 or more than 25 years
- Cadet ASP: Not less than 23 or more than 28 years

b. Height:[121]

- Male candidate: Not below 1.67 metres
- Female candidate: Not below 1.63 metres

c. Chest measurement:[122] 86 cm (for male candidates only)

d. Physical fitness:[123]

- Candidates are to be physically and mentally fit. In addition, they must be

---

[119] (Cleen.org, 2016)
<http://www.cleen.org/Report%20of%20Presidential%20Co
mmittee%20on%20Police%20Reform.pdf?> accessed 11
February 2016.
[120] ibid
[121] ibid
[122] ibid
[123] ibid

certified fit by a Government Medical Officer, before enlistment.

e. Nationality:[124]

- All candidates for enlistment into the Force must be Nigerians.

f) Educational qualification:[125]

Educational qualification for enlistment into the force are in three categories as follows:

- **Recruit Constable:** Candidates must possess at least 5 passes in the Senior Secondary School Certificate Examination. *Despite this and other requirements mentioned above, a standardized written examination for all candidates is conducted regularly in each State Command.*[126]

- **Cadet Inspector:** Candidates must possess at least 5 credits in the Senior

---

[124] ibid
[125] ibid
[126] ibid

Secondary School Certificate Examination.[127]

- **Cadet ASP:** Candidates must possess at least a degree from a University recognised by the Federal Ministry of Education.[128]

There have been rumours of corruption in police recruitment for decades in Nigeria.[129] This has produced officers that are almost illiterate and criminally minded and affiliated. But, the lack of capacity in training facilities to implement the presidential recruitment directives referenced previously grossly compromised recruitment standards (in recent memories) and resulted in large scale abuse.

Seventy percent of senior officers interviewed cannot vouch for the integrity of recruitment exercises in the police. Corruption of the

[127] ibid
[128] ibid
[129] <https://www.naij.com/557624-nigeria-police-need-repairs-says-group.html> accessed on 20 February 2016

recruitment procedure is widespread in Nigeria police, multiple sources alleges. Criminals, over - aged persons and applicants with disqualifying disabilities were all recruited. Such practices during recruitment exercise has led to the lowering of standards, across the police. The police have several internal training facilities for both new starters and ongoing development of existing officers.

4. THE TRAINING REGIME OF NEW RECRUITS.

Induction training is given to new starters to introduce them to life as police officers. The training regime and facilities for Nigeria police are however in a dreadful state.

"The institutions being used to train Nigerian police officers are decayed and cannot produce the best police officers the country needs to get better".[130] These were the words

---

[130] <http://dailytimes.com.ng/police-colleges-cant-produce-good-officers-says-aig-mbu/> accessed on 6 December 2015.

of Assistant Inspector General of police (AIG) Mr. Joseph MBU in an interview with Vanguard newspaper in November 2015.

"There is decay, there is neglect, what we have on ground is not conducive to the reform programme we all yearn for. Many projects in the training institutions have been abandoned"[131] he added. Such an indictment by a very senior police officer speaks for itself.

This research visited two police training facilities and the living conditions were very unsatisfactory. Locations of these facilities will however not be disclosed to protect sources. As the sample publicly available photographs below will show, this is not a facility fit to train animals much less police officers of a major nation.

The problems identified are multifaceted. First there is inadequate number of training places available to train the numbers being recruited.

---

[131] ibid

So short cuts are employed that leads to inadequate training and poor competence of new officers. Then there is the problem of the appalling state of the training facilities and centres. Recruits are treated like inhumanely and are taught so many bad habits that makes them accident waiting to happen upon graduation.

The parlous state of Nigerian police training facilities has been in the news in recent years. For example the police training college in Lagos was built for 700 trainees, but today it is occupied by about 2570[132] trainees. This has led to overcrowding and degraded facilities. Some buildings in this facility were built by the colonial masters in the 1940s.

The condition of most of the training facilities are not far from each other. Only facilities built recently have semblance of decorum but even these are declining due to lack of maintenance culture in Nigeria. Below are

---

[132] Figures provided by the Training college in May 2015.

pictures of the condition new recruits are being trained at the police college.

Source:
http://www.channelstv.com/2013/01/21/nigeria-police-training-expecting-something-from-nothing/

Source: http://www.osundefender.org/fg-probes-decay-in-police-colleges-others/

Source: http://www.osundefender.org/fg-probes-decay-in-police-colleges-others/

So the poor state of the training facilities is a major challenge for the police in Nigeria.

This affects the quality of new officers deployed into frontline service and if the relations with the community is to improve, there has to be a better and more conducive training facilities and regime.

Several officers spoken to in the various training facilities complain of the poor quality of new recruits. Many are much older than policy allows. Many are illiterate, with serious medical and disabling conditions and many have several children already when they join. The problem is that the names of these recruits are submitted by senior stakeholders in the police institutions and senior politicians, hence the training colleges feel compelled to accept this unsuitable recruits.

Several trainers confirmed cases of recruits with serious mental impairment being allowed to stay be senior officers. Other training instructors complained of a policy of universal passing of students regardless of their abilities.

This does not bode well for the future and the next generation of officers are already compromised from the start.

5. THE CONTINUOUS PROFESSIONAL DEVELOPMENT OF SERVING OFFICERS.

This relates to the ongoing training of serving officers as part of a continuing professional development. It also provided base training needed as prerequisites for promotion to new level.

There exist few training institutions for the officers on an ongoing basis. But the quality of the training and the support for officers attending them is questionable.

As stated previously by several of the officers interviewed for this research, it is common occurrence to ask serving officers to attend a training programme hundreds of miles away from base, but no resource is made available either for their transportation or feeding.

In the same Vanguard newspaper interview previously referenced, AIG MBU also touched on this subject by saying: *"The police profile is rising, but there is no need for course participants here to feed themselves, government should feed them to make them feel cared-for and that will, in turn, ginger them to make more sacrifice for the nation"*.[133]

The police college in Kano, became a degree awarding institution three years ago, thanks to the government of former President Goodluck Jonathan. This is a step in the right direction as it is hoped the calibre of graduating officers can only improve the police service.

But the limited number of places available at this college will need to be expanded substantially to be able to have a discernible impact of the skill and competence matrix of the serving officers throughout Nigeria. The Nigeria police Force has the following training institutions: -

a. The staff college, Jos
According to the Nigerian Open University briefing paper, *"This is the top police Training Institution. It carries out administrative and*

---

[133] ibid

command training for the officer cadre".[134] This college is headed by an Assistant Inspector General of Police.

The college helps to equip officers with management skills and capability needed to deliver its constitutional mandate.

b. The Nigeria police academy, Kano
The academy provide training for new Cadet Assistant Superintendents and Cadet Inspectors. This academy was upgraded to a degree awarding institution few years ago and its training remit expanded accordingly.

According to briefing paper by the Nigerian Open University,[135] the main objectives of the institution include:

a) The training of young university graduates who possess not less than bachelor's degree (honours) in disciplines relevant to

---

[134]

<http://www.nou.edu.ng/NOUN_OCL/pdf/SASS/CSS%2074 2.pdf?> accessed on 28 December 2015
[135] ibid

the responsibilities of the police to become Assistant Superintendent of police.[136]

b) The training of young senior secondary school leavers who possess WASC/GCE/SSC with credits in not les than five subjects including English Languages and mathematics to become Inspectors of police.[137]

c) The provision of appropriates orientation to such graduates and school certificates holders in order to imbue them with moral rectitude and sense of honour and duty.[138]

d) Producing through these schemes, a systematic chain of an incorruptible and virile police leadership with a bias for good public relationship.[139]

c. Police colleges

There exist four police Colleges located at, Kaduna, Lagos, Oji River and Maiduguri. They

---

[136] ibid
[137] ibid
[138] ibid
[139] ibid

specialise in the training of recruit constables. Some of the key courses of focus are:

i.   Inspector Promotion course
ii. Rank and File Promotion Course
iii. PC Promotion Course
iv. Basic Recruit Training
v.   Rank and File Drill Course
vi. Drivers Refresher Course
vii. Motor Maintenance Course
viii. Doron Simulator Course

d. Detective college, Enugu

This college undertakes the training of detectives and Inspectors. Majority of Inspector level officials and detectives are trained from here. programmes of the college include:[140]

i.   Anti-Fraud Course
ii. Fingerprint Course
iii. Detective Course
iv. Modus Operandi Course
v.   Prosecution Course

140

<http://www.nou.edu.ng/NOUN_OCL/pdf/SASS/CSS%2074 2.pdf?> accessed on 10th January 2016

vi.   Photographic Course

e. Foreign training

In addition to internal and external training provided within Nigeria, the police also use external training opportunities abroad. This tend to be in liaison foreign government in bilateral   agreements   or   multinational agreements.

Some of these institutions include.[141]

i.   Manchester police Training School UK

ii.   "Train the trainers" course at Harrogate UK

iii.   Senior Detective Course at Royal Mounted Police College, Ottawa

iv.   Microcomputer Orientation Course at University of Boston USA

v.   Handwriting Analysts Course in the United Kingdom

---

[141] ibid

vi.   Ballistics Course at Harrogate United Kingdom

vii.   Police Academy in Cairo for various courses.

6. EFFECT OF THE SLICING OFF OF TRADITIONAL POLICE FUNCTIONS INTO MULTIPLE ENFORCEMENT AGENCIES OUTSIDE THE COMMAND AND CONTROL OF THE NIGERIA POLICE FORCE.

The reality today in Nigeria is that many of the statutory functions of the police, have been carved out to other agencies like the Independent Corrupt Practices Commission (ICPC), the Economic and Financial Crimes Commission (EFCC), Federal Roads Safety Commission (FRSC), and the Nigerian Security and Civil Defence Corps (NSCDC) .

This challenge was discussed in the previous chapter in terms of the financial implications of these agencies. Other than political exigencies, there appears to be no logical reasoning for the establishment of so many duplicating agencies in law enforcement.

All these multiple agencies consume resources that could be used for core policing work. This was discussed in the previous chapter. It is difficult to see how the main Nigeria police can function effectively against the background of these duplicating agencies.

Based on this research, the main challenges with recruitment and training facing the Nigerian police can be summarized as follows:

1) *Inadequate Funding for world class police training.*

This research discovered sparsely furnished police training facilities, with inadequate facilities, (both for training and hostels), a theoretically focused training regime with not enough practical element. A newly trained officer told this researcher for instance of having just passed out of an officer training class being taught on scientific investigatory technics but never actually performing any scientific experiments or tests.

All was based on textbook study of theories, which he committed to memory and regurgitated at his exam to pass. How effective will such an officer be in practice?

2) *Lack of transparent training related promotion criteria.*

On paper, an officer is supposed to have attended certain number of specified training before he or she can be promoted to certain ranks in the police.

But allegedly due to corruption and nepotism, many officers are given accelerated promotions above their peers despite having not attended the specified training for that rank and many are promoted despite having serious allegations of misconduct still unresolved.[142]

This demotivates officers who largely believe that promotion is purely a political exercise of "who you know at the top" rather than a meritorious exercise in competency. Eighty percent of the officers interviewed believe that merit alone will not get you promoted in the Nigerian police.

This affects the attitude of many officer to police training as useless or as a necessary evil, rather than being a developmental exercise to increase competence and operational effectiveness. This reduces the impact of the training on the officers that attend.

3) *Lack of visible nexus between training and better policing.*

---

[142] 'Promoting Corruption and Misconduct In The Nigeria Police | Sahara Reporters' (Sahara Reporters, 2016) <http://www.saharareporters.com/2013/01/24/promoting-corruption-and-misconduct-nigeria-police> accessed 11 February 2016.

Ninety-five percent of the general public interviewed considers the problem of corruption in the police to be at an all time high. Also, eighty-five percent of people questioned believe there is no clear link between more training and better behaved police officers on the street. This disconnect has called into question the quality of the training offered to the officers.

With more training seems to come more corrupt practices and oppression of the citizenry. Even sixty percent of officers questions say that they do not see their ongoing training as having effectively prepared them for life in the frontline. So many have concluded that the training is not working.

4) Poor quality of training.

The Nigerian media from time to time feature stories of students in universities as well as officers in training colleges bribing their teachers to ensure they pass examinations. This is an endemic problem in Nigeria as a whole.

So fifty-five percent of officers interviewed admitted to paying their lecturers to ensure they pass examinations and tests at police training facilities. Another twenty percent admitted to using the influence of "god fathers" and known superior officers to pressurised trainers to achieve the same outcome as bribery. This is a serious crisis of wasted training effort.

This calls into question the quality of the training being offered and its rigour and effectiveness. It is not uncommon to meet police officers at checkpoints who cannot read English, yet they have supposedly passed out of police training facilities.

From trainees interviewed and the observation of this researcher in facilities visited, there is evidence of an emphasis on the hard side of policing at police training facilities.

Too much focus seems to be given to use of weapons, crowd control and other control mechanism and less on negotiation, respect for human rights and humane treatment of suspects.

This adds credence to the perceived believe of the historical militarization of the police.

5) Inadequate number of training places
The ambition of the politicians to recruit more officers is not matched by the number of training places available for new recruits. A senior police source told this research that when the former President Obasanjo announced in 2001, a drive to recruit 40,000 police officers annually during his regime, this could not be actualized because the training places available annually in all police recruit training facilities was for about 32% of that figure.

So there is need for expansion of training places if more officers are to be trained properly to fight crime in the country.

6) Non compliance with recruitment criteria

With constant media reports of nepotism and favouritism in police recruitment, senior police sources told this researcher that up to 90% of new recruits get accepted due to referral from other police officers. These tend to be their friends and relatives, many not qualified but could not be turned down due to pressure from superior ranks.

Once accepted these officers will continue to be protected from discipline by their 'god-fathers' in the force, thus institutionalizing mediocrity and poor performance. When asked, eighty percent of police officers interviewed by this research confirm they have witnessed or heard of this practice of non-compliance with policy.

7) Lack of proper vetting of Recruits

Nigeria has no centralized criminal records agency. There also exist no national Credit Bureau either. So sources spoken to by this research claimed that vetting candidates objectively is very difficult. Additionally, the basics like collecting references, medical and psychiatric examinations are not done in many instances.

It is not uncommon for new recruits to be in their 30s or even 40s and with many children already. This is clearly against policy but it happens all the time in Nigeria. The poor vetting of new intakes has helped create a steady pipeline of criminal and unsuitable new officers within the police.

8) Lack of appeal or attraction of police job

Many parents do not want their children becoming police officers due to its poor reputation and regard by the communities as well as its poor remuneration and conditions of service and welfare. This means children of VIPs and respectable national figures tend not to join the police. The force therefore tends to attract criminal elements who then use the police to commit further crimes and oppress the population claimed sources spoken to.

9) General lack of Meritocracy.

It is a pervasive believe among servicing frontline officers that if you don't have a "godfather" in the superior ranks you will not progress in your police career. Ninety percent of the officers interviewed agreed that you need a "godfather" if you are to make good progress in your policing career.

This has led to a collapse in meritocracy and nepotism and influence peddling is the order of the day. There are cases of officers who people expect to be dismissed for breach of the rules being promoted instead of disciplined.

In his journal contribution, Emmanuel C. Onyeozili, lamented on the obstacles facing the Nigeria police by stating that:

"In Nigeria, it is common knowledge that the higher echelon of the military and the police, is dominated by particular sections of the country, and promotions often follow the same pattern. Within the police, protégés are appointed to head the departments they are not qualified to hold, while career-minded officers are posted to police "Siberia" for not "playing ball". The dismissed IG, Tafa Balogun, is said to have promoted his driver (whom he uses as front in his extortion of money from state commissioners of police) to Chief Security Officer (CSO), while some state commissioners were redeployed for not bringing in enough kickbacks (The News, 2003)".[143]

---

[143] Onyeozili, Emmanuel C. "Obstacles to effective policing in Nigeria." *African Journal of Criminology and Justice Studies: AJCJS* 1.1 (2005): 32.

A practical example is the case of the police Commissioner, Mr Mbu of the Rivers state police command. He clashed with the Governor of the state who is the Chief Security Officer of the state.[144] There is a perception by many that Mbu crossed the line of politeness and impartiality by seeming to overtly supporting the governing political party.

The facts in this public acrimony between the two public officials are not fully clear for the public to make informed decision. However, not very long after the clash and public spat, Mbu was promoted to an Assistant Inspector General of police.

A reward many participants questioned perceived was for his partisan loyalty to the governing party in 2013. There are other allegations of unmerited support and promotion of offending officers. Those who

---

[144] <http://www.premiumtimesng.com/news/top-news/168189-amaechi-mbu-in-fresh-war-of-words.html> accessed on 15 January 2016

do not have "Godfathers" simply bribe their way through the police bureaucracy. In fact in early 2016, the Senate Committee on Police Affairs started an hearing into reported irregularities and favouritism in recent police promotion exercises.[145]

In an article in Daily Independent newspaper, Dr Chucks Osuji, lamented the rot in the police by stating that:

> "Some policemen pay heavy bribe for them to be posted to the Southern parts of the Nigeria like: Aba, Port Harcourt, Owerri, Onitsha, Lagos, Ibadan and Benin City. These were considered to be crime-ridden areas with "trouble-makers" where police are very busy. And this could be translated into "cash". In fact, it has been alleged that police men do everything possible to avoid being posted to the North

---

[145] <http://www.dailytrust.com.ng/news/general/senate-probes-arase-s-lopsided-promotions-in-police/126493.html> accessed on 15 March 2016

because it is not a fertile area for troubles".[146]

Osuji further posited that:

"In addition, other privileges and incentives available for police officers are corruptly distributed. Sadly enough, corruptive discrimination is heavily alleged in the police. Many claim that only those who have Abraham as a father get rapid promotions, considered for any juicy posting and are favoured regularly, while those bereft of such Abraham watch in frustration as their colleagues pass them on as if they are not in the same force. The cumulative of this state of affairs is that the morale in the police is very low, indeed. And if this is added to the disdain with which our police is treated, often these officers fail to rise to the occasion when

---

[146] <http://dailyindependentnig.com/2012/07/nigeria-police-most-misunderstood-under-rated-and-vilified-why-2/> accessed on 15 January 2016

expected to "die for the nation". They may seem to ask, "die for which nation? Die for which people?"[147]

This lack of meritocracy feeds into the widespread allegation of corruption against the police. Many officers influence and bribe their way into being posted to areas they believe they can make more money rather than where they can best serve the public.

---

[147] ibid

Chapter SIX

RECOMMENDATIONS FOR DEVELOPING GOOD GOVERNANCE IN THE NIGERIAN POLICE

There have been many opinions declared on the challenges facing the Nigeria police by many scholars some of whom have been identified in previous chapters.

There have been challenges explained in some detail and other mentioned superficially. But truly there can be no solution to the many institutional problems facing the police without examining *the credentials and operational status of the individual police officer.*

Who gets to wear the uniform? What background does he/she have? What training have they received? What support does he/she get on the job? The questions are endless. But these questions underscore the need to investigate thoroughly the antecedents of persons hired into the police force.

Therefore, the recommendations in this research will focus and be targeted at three main players or themes:

1) The individual police officer

2) The Institution of the police force as a whole

3) The interactions and operational relationships between the Government, the police and the community.

In addition, the recommendations in this chapter will be restricted to those that relate to the two areas of challenges considered in Chapters 4 and 5. Additionally, this research is basing its recommendations on the continuing centralised federal police structure in Nigeria.

Based on the findings, it is the conclusion of this research that Nigeria is not yet ripe for state policing based on the current unitary governance that exist in Nigeria.

Of course as part of a politically restructured nation, some state policing will become inevitable. It is also needful to state that there will always be need for a federal police institution in Nigeria; even in a fully restructured federation. This is due to the fact that some crimes will need to be federally processed due to its character and peculiar facts.

The political maturity and unified environment needed for state policing to thrive does not currently exist in Nigeria. With threats of breakaway and regional agitations as well as rampant ethnic strife, the enabling environment for such segregated policing structure does not exist in Nigeria. However, if there is a decision to restructure the governance of the federation the structure and governance of the police will have to be part of that settlement. More on this subject will be examined in the second volume of this book.

The recommendations in this Chapter will be classed into three areas as follows:

1) Recommendations in relation to the Financial and Budgetary challenges facing the Nigeria police.
2) Recommendations in relation to the Recruitment and Training challenges facing the Nigeria police.
3) Additional Recommendations that do not fit fully within either of the above two areas.

1. RECOMMENDATIONS IN RELATION TO THE FINANCIAL AND BUDGETARY

CHALLENGES FACING THE NIGERIAN POLICE.

SALARIES, ALLOWANCES AND WELFARE

Research Finding: The salary and welfare packages that serving and retired police officers get does not seen to reflect the scale of the task they perform for the public. The risks, the irregular and long hours and other terms and condition is not at a level that reflects the unique danger the police are exposed to in Nigeria.

Also, the police is grouped together with the wider civil service in terms of pay levels, so the government is afraid that any special increase in police pay could trigger the same agitation by the rest of the civil service, thus increasing the overhead of the government. Just like the military are on a different pay scale from the rest of government employees, the police should be considered for similar benefit.

This has led many police officers to seek to supplement their income through corrupt practices. Therefore, the current pay and allowances of the police are unfair, especially considering the risk involved in the job. Also, many of the inefficiencies and misconduct seen within the police can be traced to poor pay and conditions.

Ninety percent of serving officers interviewed feel unappreciated by both the government and the general public. Hence a feeling develops where an officer feels *"if I don't look after myself, nobody will…nobody cares about what happens to me"* as stated by sixty-five percent of responding officers.

RECOMMENDATION 1:

A distinct Salary Scale for the police outside of the unified public service pay scales should be created to reflect the full scale of the work being done by the police in Nigeria. Eighty percent of the people interviewed by this research recommends a minimum of 100% increase in the starting basic pay of the police to about N108,000. This research agrees with and recommends this level of increase.

Exact figures for the West African sub region is difficult to obtain. It seems however to be mixed picture with many countries having a unified pay scale for their police and other having a special pay scale.

For example, Ghana introduced a new Single Spine Salary Structure (SSSS) for its police in 2010. The SSSS had a built in premium for the special risks involved in police work. This saw an increase in pay that officers were happy with.[148]

Public service must never be just about the financial benefit, So the police should not be exempted from this well established ethos of service to the country. Any increase above this recommended level could make money

---

[148] 'Police Service Satisfied with New Pay Policy - IGP' (Ghanaweb.com, 2016) <http://www.ghanaweb.com/GhanaHomePage/NewsArchive/Police-service-satisfied-with-new-pay-policy-IGP-187423> accessed 11 February 2016.

the overwhelming reason for joining and this will not be good. The one hundred percentage increase recommended seem to strike the right balance.

Ninety-five percent of officers interviewed believe an increase of this magnitude will go along way to discourage survival/subsistence related corruption within the force, thus allowing for the hard core really corrupt officers to be exposed. This increase should then be cascaded upwards to all ranks.

The table below lists the monthly pay of some of the key posts in the police force and recommended increase.

	RANK	Approximate Current starting Monthly Salary[149]	Approximate Recommended Starting Basic Salary (100% Increase)
	TRAINING POSITIONS	(N)	(N)
1	Recruit	9,019	18,038
	OPERATIONAL RANKS		
2	Constable (Grade level 03 -10)	43,293 – 51,113	86,586 – 102,226
3	Corporal (Grade level 01 – 10)	44,715 – 51,113	89,430 – 102,226
4	Sergeant (Grade 5, Step 1 to 10)	48,540 – 55,973	97,080 – 111,946
5	Sergeant Major	62,204	124,408
6	Cadet Inspector (Grade level 7, Step 1-10)	73,231 – 87,135	146,462 – 174,270
7	Assistant Superintendent	127,604 – 144,152	255,208 – 288,304

---

[149] <http://www.nigerianbulletin.com/threads/nigerian-police-force-salary-structure.197574/> accessed on 04 April 2016

	RANK	Approximate Current starting Monthly Salary[149]	Approximate Recommended Starting Basic Salary (100% Increase)
	(Grade 8, Step 1 – 10)		
8	Assistant Superintendent (Grade 9, Step 1 – 10)	136,616 – 156,318	273,232 – 312,636
9	Deputy Superintendent (Grade 10, Step 1 – 10)	148,733 – 170,399	297,466 – 340,798
10	Superintendent (Grade 11, Step 1-10)	161,478 – 187,616	322,956 – 375,232
11	Chief Superintendent (Grade 12, step 1 – 8)	172,089 – 199,723	344,178 – 399,446
12	Assistant Commissioner (Grade 13, step 10)	212,938	425,876

	RANK	Approximate Current starting Monthly Salary[149]	Approximate Recommended Starting Basic Salary (100% Increase)
13	Deputy Commissioner (Grade 14, step 7)	278,852	557,704
14	Commissioner (Grade 15)	302,970	605,940
15	Assistant Inspector-General (Grade 16, step5)l	546,572	1,093,144
16	Inspector-General	711,498	1,422,996

Figure 15: Some of the police current[150] and recommended salaries

RECOMMENDATION 2:

It is recommended that allowances of officers should be increased across the board by 50% to help support officers in the line of duty.

---

[150] ibid

Some (but not all) of the known allowances are:

- Accommodation
- Medical
- Transport
- Meal Subsidy
- Utility
- Training
- Hazard Allowance
- Uniform and maintenance Allowance

RECOMMENDATION 3:

All Allowances due to officers MUST be paid prior to their departure as applicable and not during or after.

So officers set on a course should be paid ALL their allowance before they depart for their training, while officers should be paid their due allowances prior to departure on transfer.

This recommendation is due to the fact that all senior police officers spoken to at divisional level, confirmed these allowances either never being paid at all and when paid months or even years in arrears. The prompt payment will seek to encourage and motivate the officers.

RECOMMENDATION 4:

Currently, there is no certain mechanism for negotiating any potential pay dispute or seek improvement of service within the police. It is recommended that an Independent Pay Review Body be established to administer the new police Pay Scale that will be introduced.

As police officers in Nigeria are prohibited by law from embarking on strike (industrial action), an independent pay review body will better ensure credibility of recommendations and fairness of the process.

RECOMMENDATION 5:

In several jurisdictions, the police are permitted to be part of unions and federations, thus helping to stimulate professionalism and support the welfare of officers. While the law banning strike action by the police should remain in force, it is recommended that the police be legally permitted to form an association or federation to afford officers a channel for collective bargaining.

Where there are unresolved matters between the new police federation/union and the new pay review body in collective bargaining, there shall be a recourse to Nigeria's Industrial Arbitration Panel and the National Industrial Court as applicable

RECOMMENDATION 6:

As part of a new welfare push for the police, it is recommended that proper Medicare care should be provided to all police officers. In theory, all serving police officers are already entitled to free medical care as part of their condition of service.

But in practice, most officers pay for their own medical care as well as their families even for those who sustained injuries in the line of duty. Most State police Commands have police clinics but they are mostly understaffed and under equipped.

Therefore, all current police treatment centres need to be upgraded, equipped and properly staffed to serve the needs of serving officers. In addition, police officers and their families should be registered under the new National Health Insurance Scheme to allow them free (government funded) access to specialist medical care not available at police clinics.

If necessary, a maximum contribution of 1% of basic salary should be made by officers to benefit from the wider and specialist treatment provisions covered by the National Health Insurance Scheme.

ALLOCATION AND MANAGEMENT OF POLICE BUDGET

Research Finding: This research found that the process of budgeting in the police is top down rather than bottom up. Hence a lot of the needs at the local level are not adequately reflected in approved budgets.

Also there is an absence of sustained multi-year strategic planning in the police. Everything seem to just be on a year by year basis. There is clear lack of medium term planning.

There is a general confusion and mystery around the exact total funds spent by the police each year. This is due to the many sources of funding earlier explained and listed in Chapter 5, some of which are not publicly revealed.

The headquarters of the police control 70 per cent of the allocated federal budget. This creates shortages of fund at the state command level due to mismanagement and corruption at the headquarters.

RECOMMENDATION 7:

It is recommended that the police authorities should produce as a minimum, a five-year strategic plan, that will itemise its funding requirements and operational strategy over that period.

The budgets allocated will therefore track this plan and allow for multi-year settlement to be possible. The era of reactive annual fire fighting must come to an end. This will enable the government to spread its funding of the police in ways that allows for the normal up and down of public finances.

RECOMMENDATION 8:

It is recommended that the operational budget to each state command should be disbursed directly to the Commissioner heading each state. The police headquarters should henceforth manage only budgets that directly relates to its own running cost and any interstate or centralised police needs.

The disbursement of local budgets and its management should be left to the state Commissioners to control and manage. This will stop the current state of affairs where the headquarter is seen as a bottleneck thus restricting the efficient flow of funds to the states.

RECOMMENDATION 9:

As a matter of public policy, a law should be enacted giving all serving police officers free travel privileges on all government (local, state and federal) owned transportation systems (with the exception of air travel).

This will ease the operational movement of the police, but also reduce the transportation budget of the police or at least make the funds available go further.

FUNDING OF INFRASTRUCTURE, INTELLIGENCE GATHERING AND FACILITIES

Research Findings: In many states, it has been the goodwill of state governments, charities and well meaning individuals that has allowed police stations to be somehow habitable and sparsely furnished. Funding for office refits and refurbishment rarely come from the police headquarters.

These poor facilities sap morale and lower the esteem of the police in the eyes of the public. It also discourages the public from visiting police stations to report crime or offer intelligence to the police.

RECOMMENDATION 10:

The government should immediately make funding available as part of a strategic intervention portfolio funding to commence the refurbishment and rebuilding of police posts, stations and operational centres across the federation. This should be on a roll in basis over an agreed period, maybe 7years.

Such improved facilities will support good operational practices as the police fulfil their constitutional mandate to protect the public and detect and prosecute crime.

OPERATIONAL FINANCIAL CHALLENGES

Research Findings: The research found that good policing usually tends to revolve around certain key factors namely: Trainable manpower, Transportation, Communication and Logistic support.

Nigeria is a country of 924,000 square kilometres with over 167million people.[151] The rapid urbanisation creating city sprawls and villages reducing in population as a result of labour migration, the job of policing modern Nigeria is daunting and challenging.

---

[151] 'Nigeria Country Profile - BBC News' (BBC News, 2016) <http://www.bbc.co.uk/news/world-africa-13949550> accessed 11 February 2016.

TRANSPORTATION

This research found that there are over 12,000 police formations nationwide requiring transportation day and night to operation efficiently. The primary duty of the police is maintenance of law and order and protecting the residents of Nigeria.

The police are currently failing to fulfil their constitutional mandate in many areas as a result of poor infrastructure and facilities. Fifty percent of police officers interviewed said their stations do not have functioning patrol vehicle. This research was further told that many police stations and even divisions have no patrol or operational vehicles in some states. Sixty-five percent of the public questioned stated that they have had experience of calling the police in an emergency only to be told there is no vehicle to respond to the emergency in the past five years.

And on the odd occasions when there was a vehicle, the police will say there is no petrol in the car claimed another twenty percent of the public.

MARINE DIVISION

The research also found a neglect of the police marine division, with dilapidated facilities and non provision of boats and launches and other facilities.

This is despite the fact that 21 of the 36 states in Nigeria have riverine terrains. With oil theft, vandalism and bunkering costing the nation Billions of dollars, the ill-equipped police force cannot fulfil their constitutional mandate.

COMMUNICATIONS

Effective communication is an essential part of modern policing. This allows interconnectivity between the field and the base. It also allows the police to monitor criminals adequately. And in a world of modern IT technology, criminals use all manner of ways to evade the police and some even monitor police communications.

In this regard, many criminals have an edge over the police with their more sophisticated communication equipment. The following represents the list of communication equipment possessed by the police based on the data given to this research by police sources in October 2015.

1	Fax Machine	95
2	Ultra High Frequency Mobile	415
3	Ultra High Frequency Walkie Talkie	6,702
4	High Frequency Radio	317
5	Ultra High Frequency Base	380

6	Ultra High Frequency Repeaters	78
7	Solar Panel	51
8	Aerial Masts	189

Figure 16: Police communication inventory[152]

For operational excellence, each police officer is supposed to be equipped with a walkie talkie. If so, that will mean over 360,000 walkie talkie units in operation. The Nigerian police have only 6,702 units. Also with 774 local government areas supposed to be equipped with a high frequency radio each, the police have only 317, thus leaving more than half the country not covered as far as communication is concerned.

The communication equipment is not standardised across the police force. Senior police sources interviewed for this research

---

[152] Data provided by three senior police sources x, y and z (anonymity preserved) and the CLEEN Foundation Resource Centre Lagos.

lamented that the staff employed to operate communications equipment tend to be low level technicians, instead of efficient professionals.

ICT

The use of Information and Communication Technology by the police is an essential requirement for effective law enforcement all the world. The Nigeria police is lagging behind with many police station in the country not having any computer equipment whatsoever.

In Western nations, the police have established formidable crime detection and fighting tools with the help of ICT. Some of the common tools are:

1. National Crime database
2. Criminal Record Bureau, (like in the UK).
3. Centralised Crime Information Centre
4. Automated fingerprints Identification Systems (AFIS)

None of these is operational in the Nigerian police.

HIGH v LOW POLICING[153]

Nigerian police focus too much on 'Low" policing at the expense of "High Policing. Low policing refers to the everyday routine protection of citizens. This is largely reactive policing based on either notification of ongoing criminality or after the criminal act have been committed. High policing on the other hand refers to matters threatening to the security of the state.

This tend to be pro-active activities like surveillance, intelligence gathering and undercover infiltration of the criminal communities. This is not to say that the Nigerian police do the low policing well either. It is just that the high policing is largely non existent as a practice. The skills, competence, capacity and funds required for sustained high

---

[153] J Brodeur, (1983) ' High Policing and Low Policing', *Social Problems*, 30/5: 507-20.

level policing is not present in the police as currently constituted.

RECOMMENDATION 11:

It is recommended that a statutory requirement of a minimum of one working patrol vehicle per police station should be enacted. If the number of police station need to be reduced to make this happen, that will be acceptable, especially in urban areas when many stations are not far from each other.

Without a working vehicle, a police station cannot provide effective response to emergencies, thus failing in its constitutional mandate to protect.

RECOMMENDATION 12:

It is recommended that funds should be provided to fully equip the marine division of the police, as this will pay for itself in savings from reduction in oil theft by criminals. This will involve the purchase of landing crafts, personnel launchers as well as the construction of coastal jetties

RECOMMENDATION 13:

It is recommended that as a priority there should be the provision of secured voice communications system for the Nigerian police. It is recommended that a Digital Radio System be procured and implemented that meets global standard of digital communication.

RECOMMENDATION 14:

It is recommended that the computerisation of the police should be implemented as a priority. This should involve but not limited to the computerisation of the following:

i.   Police Pay Rolls
ii.   Crime records and central Intelligence register
iii. Central Motor Registry
iv.   Criminal /Offenders records across all the states
v.   Logistics/Asset Register. This should include fixed and movable assets like properties to Armoury and vehicles.

RECOMMENDATION 15:

It is recommended that both the Ministry of police affairs and the Police Service Commission should be abolished. They are not effective and their existence creates duplicated cost centres for the government.

A new Agency should be created that will combine the performance monitoring and complaints investigation roles.

- This new agency should have Ministerial oversight from the existing Internal Affairs ministry.
- The new agency should be chaired by a person not connected to the police and have majority non-police members.
- The power to dismiss officers must rest with this new agency.

RECOMMENDATION 16:

Because the operational needs of the police formations are similar in nature, they should be made to pool their procurement needs together to enjoy economies of scale.

So neighbouring police commands should be encouraged to procure together back office needs and items not centrally procured by the headquarters at the moment.

RECOMMENDATION 17:

To save cost and strengthen the police, it is recommended that the State Security Service (SSS), EFCC, CCB, NDLEA, FRSC, ICPC, National Civil Defence Corps and the Vehicle Inspector Office (VIO) should be merged with the Nigerian police immediately. To maintain expertise and focus, they can be made departments under the police structure. But a unified headship will provide for better joined up thinking, save cost on back office functions and increase overall funding to the police.

For instance, as previously noted in chapter 5, the SSS was until the mid 70s part of the police but known as the Special Branch. This amalgamation of all policing related agencies will also simplify law enforcement hierarchy for Nigerians. Currently it is not unusual for citizens to report same crime to multiple policing agencies out of confusion of who exactly is responsible for investigation.

The new bigger police will also create economies of scale with its procurement that will ensure greater efficiency and best value is achieved. This will also bolster the High Level policing capability of the police immensely.

Additionally, this amalgamation will stop the current trend where there are officers wearing all manner of uniforms on the road and on the street from all these agencies. This always create confusion as to which agency they are.

For example there was a public spat few years ago between the police and FRSC on who should issue and maintain drivers licence to motorists in Nigeria.[154] In fact, at one point

---

[154]   <http://www.vanguardngr.com/2012/03/number-plate-drivers-licence-drama-as-frsc-police-disagree-over-registration/> accessed on 2 February 2016

both agencies presented their own version of drivers' licence to the confusion of the general public. The Senate had to intervene to resolve the problem.

This public row further supports the fact that too many agencies are performing policing related duties which is unconstitutional. Like the saying goes, if it looks like a dog, barks like a dog, walk like a dog, then it is a dog. The fact that these agencies are not called police is irrelevant.

The Nigerian Constitution states clearly as noted in Chapter 5 that there shall be only one police force in Nigeria and it is to be federally controlled. The fact as stated already that many of these agencies were carved out of the previous police force, proves the point that they should return to the police force so that Nigerian police can become strengthened, well funded, joined up and unified police institution.

Most countries in the Anglophone West African countries have a unified police structure, but the Francophone countries have layers of policing agencies after the French system.

RECOMMENDATION 18:

Inter-Agency cooperation should be mandated. A joint intelligence platform or system should be created with other law enforcement agencies to enable a unified assessment of threats and risks to national security.

This will require the pulling together of intelligence from the Military Intelligence directorate, the State Security Service (if it remains a separate agency) and Department of State Security.

The intelligence should be graded accordingly to allow for different level of access classification on the principle of Need to Know and should the reflect the various clearance levels of police officers.

RECOMMENDATION 19:

Investment should be provided to establish a world class national Forensic Laboratory for the police. This should be staffed by high trained individuals. The practice of sending sample abroad for testing should stop. As the biggest economy in Africa, Nigeria should become the destination and partner of choice for other countries.

RECOMMENDATION 20:

Other than elected senior officials, police security should be withdrawn from all VIPs and wealthy individuals. As noted in Chapter 6, up to 40 per cent of serving police officers are tied down as private security for VIPs. But with a flourishing private security sector, these VIPs should employ their own private security and release police officers to do frontline duty to deliver on their constitutional mandate to the public.

This will release about 100,000 officers to perform frontline police duties. A new licensing system should be developed to grade private security firms from basic to advanced firms.

Basic rated will allow for basic security provision and Advanced will require practitioners to be fully vetted and allowed to carry arms as a result. This will reduce pressure on police to perform personal security roles for the wealthy.

RECOMMENDATION 21:
It is recommended that resources should be provided to train and equip the police with High level police capabilities. This will strengthen surveillance and intelligence gathering work needed to pro actively detect and deter criminality across the nation.

RECOMMENDATIONS IN RELATION TO THE RECRUITMENT AND TRAINING CHALLENGES FACING THE NIGERIA POLICE.

TRAINING, RETENTION AND RECRUITMENT

Research Findings: As detailed in Chapter 5, Nigerian police recruitment exercises and practices are blighted with corrupt practices that allows unsuitable individuals to be employed. There is also lack of security of tenure for the Inspector General of police which makes them easier to politically influence and manipulate.

Nigeria has had ten Inspector Generals of Police in ten years. This makes the IGPs more susceptible to external influence by the government as the President does the hiring and firing of IGPs as he pleases. This was discussed in detailed in Chapter Four.

Inequity in promotion exercises within the police has led to many officers feeling frustrated due to lack of promotion. Many officers remain in same rank for over a decade and with no disciplinary record.

Seventy percent of officers interviewed said they know at least a colleague that has been affected by this. From respondents' responses it would appear that this scenario is most rampant amongst the Sergeant to Inspector ranks.

Also the training regime of the police is not robust and places emphasis more on the physical aspect of the job rather than the intellectual aspect.

A very senior source told this researcher that most of lecturers at the police colleges training recruits do not have recognised teaching qualifications or training. Many are serving operational officers redeployed to training duties. Others have been training for a long time but still no training qualification. Consequently, many do not know how to teach. Postings of serving officers to training duties is seen as a punishment rather than a prestige and an opportunity to shape the future.

This lack of effective teaching knowledge handicaps the students understanding and knowledge impartation. The very bad reputation of the police means many of the stakeholders in the country and key influencers do not allow their family members to join. Thus the police do not reflect the wide range of the demography and socio-cultural classes of the country.

As with previous recommendations above, some of these recommendations will require legislative changes to the Police Act as applicable. The Constitutional rights and roles of the police remain unchanged; however, a constitutional amendment will be needed to abolish some name agencies.

RECOMMENDATION 22:

It is recommended that the Inspector Generals of Police should serve a defined tenure (for example a four-year term) except in the case of gross misconduct. The President should no longer have the final say on the dismissal of IGPs.

All the president should do is nominate and as customary, it is for the Senate to confirm the candidate.

- The Senate should should hold confirmation hearings to confirm or reject such appointments thus providing democratic oversight of the process.
- Consequently, a similar majority vote by the senate must be obtained if the President wants to dismiss an IGP before his term ends. The current practice of single handed dismissal by the president only serve to make the IGP beholding to the president and more susceptible to political influence. The IGP should be able to rest in the assurance that if he applies the law impartially, he will be safe in his job, even if it does not favour the party in power.
- An IGP's term can always be renewed at the end of his/her tenure if needed.

RECOMMENDATION 23:

There should be urgent amendment of Sections 215 and 216 of the Constitution. This should address three main areas of concern:

1. The IGP should be provided with a constitutional pathway to challenge any unlawful direction from the president.

2. The Constitution should be amended to abolish the moribund Nigeria Police Council that is virtually a non operational body.

3. There also should be a change in the law to allow non police officers to become IGP. This post should be open to anybody that can meet the defined specification.

For the first time in the nation's history of democratic governance as an example, the current Comptroller General of the Nigerian

Customs service was appointed from outside the rank and file[155].

This appointment[156] is considered by many to be a stroke of genius as the new head has starting shaking and transforming the service. This is a sign of what is possible if the IGP position is made available to a wider pool of applicants.

Qualified people from the criminal justice system for instance can be excellent IGPs and be more effective in bringing fresh eyes to long standing challenges that an internal candidate may not be able to see.

RECOMMENDATION 24:

It is recommended that there should be clearly defined promotion criteria, with an appeal process for dissatisfied officers. The burden

---

155

<https://www.customs.gov.ng/About/management_team.php> accessed on 10 February 2016

156 <http://shipsandports.com.ng/buhari-appoints-retired-army-colonel-as-new-customs-cg/> accessed on 10 February 2016

should be statutorily put on the police authorities to explain why an officer has not been promoted based on the guidelines.

In addition, the number of public praise and compliments for an officer as well as complaints should be taken into account when promotion is being considered. So simply serving a defined number of years alone should not qualify an officer for promotion, but the wider contest of quality of service to the public should be considered as well.

RECOMMENDATION 25:

A complete overhaul of the training syllabus and emphasis of the police is recommended. There is need for greater emphasis on criminal law and procedures, rules of evidence and understanding fully the role of the police in the criminal justice system.

Dispute resolution and mediation should also be made standard items on the training syllabus. Training of officers need to emphasis 'procedural fairness' for all as key to winning public confidence and entrenching good governance.

It is noted here that the upgrade of the police academy to a degree awarding institution three years ago is welcomed.

But policing study should be made more readily available in Nigerian universities as a degree subject. This will allow more people to be training simultaneously than the limited space available in the police academy.

RECOMMENDATION 26:

It is recommended that the police move away from manual/paper production of case files to an electronic based process. This will involve fresh training for all officers.

- This can be rolled out in phases with pilot of the system in certain state command areas.
- A private sector sponsored pilot is a possibility.

- This will require supply of computer hardware and back-up power supply units to each police station and posts.

RECOMMENDATION 27:

It is recommended that the starting qualification for all police recruits should be a University degree or Polytechnic HND. This will enhance the status of the police and policing to a respected profession.

- All existing officers without a degree should be encouraged and supported to get qualification through institutions like the Open University of Nigeria that is on a part time basis and others. They should be given six years to acquire this qualification. Those who do not meet up should be retired at the end of this period or moved to a wholly back office duty.

- With the significant pay and conditions increases recommended in Recommendation 1 above, more qualified police personnel is required.

RECOMMENDATION 28:

There should be an introduction of a **teaching certification programme** for all teachers at the police colleges. This can be developed in conjunction with some Nigerian universities. Only those that have obtained such teaching qualification should be allowed to teach at the police colleges.

There should also be more use of visiting lecturers from within and outside Nigeria to enhance the quality of knowledge pool available to the recruits.

- Alongside the certification programme, there should be a better training regime for serving officers. As the saying goes, garbage in is garbage out, so officers that are not well trained or who are provided on the job development training too late and less frequently will be terrible teachers once sent to the police colleges.

  So senior officers should be training more often and more rigorously if they are to add any value to the training capability of the police.

RECOMMENDATION 29:

An emphasis of the Ethics of Policing should be made a compulsory and standing item in all continuing police training programme for new and serving officers. Officers need to constantly be reminded of the need for ethical behaviour and practices. This should also be linked a development and promotion of a new visible Code of Ethics of the police.

This code should be highly publicised so that all the citizenry are aware as well as all police officers. In fact, officers should be made to carry a small cade with these ethical codes along with their Identity cards at all times. Also all serving officers must be made to sign this new code of ethics, if they are to keep their job.

A world-renowned recognisable reference point that is canvassed whenever a call is made to reform policing in the Western

Europe is what has come to be known as 'Peel's principles'.[157] This could be a starting point for the Nigerian version.

These principles are expressed in his famous nine points as follows:[158]

1) The basic mission for which the police exist is to prevent crime and disorder.[159]

2) The ability of the police to perform their duties is dependent upon public approval of police actions.[160]

3) Police must secure the willing co-operation of the public in voluntary observance of the law to be able to secure and maintain the respect of the public.[161]

---

[157] C Emsley, (2013) 'Peel's Principles, Police Principles', in J. Brown (ed) *The Future of Policing*. London: Routledge.
[158] 'Peel's "Nine Points" Of Policing' (Historyhome.co.uk, 2016)
<http://www.historyhome.co.uk/peel/laworder/9points.htm> accessed 11 March 2016.
[159] ibid
[160] ibid
[161] ibid

4) The degree of co-operation of the public that can be secured diminishes proportionately to the necessity of the use of physical force.[162]

5) Police seek and preserve public favour not by catering to public opinion but by constantly demonstrating absolute impartial service to the law.[163]

6) Police use physical force to the extent necessary to secure observance of the law or to restore order only when the exercise of persuasion, advice and warning is found to be insufficient.[164]

7) Police, at all times, should maintain a relationship with the public that gives reality to the historic tradition that the police are the public and the public are the police; the police being only members of the public who are paid to give full-time attention to duties which are incumbent on every citizen in the

---

[162] ibid
[163] ibid
[164] ibid

interests of community welfare and existence.[165]

8) Police should always direct their action strictly towards their functions and never appear to usurp the powers of the judiciary.[166]

9) The test of police efficiency is the absence of crime and disorder, not the visible evidence of police action in dealing with it.[167]

These principles are historical, generic and they do not fully reflect the vitality of Constitutional rights as well as the prevalence of technology driven criminality of modern era.

But it is a good place to start for the Nigerian police as it can be tweaked and made bespoke to meet its esoteric needs and constitutional mandate to protect.

---

[165] ibid
[166] ibid
[167] ibid

RECOMMENDATION 30:

The authorities should establish the use of online reporting platform for crime reporting. All police officers should be trained in the use of modern technology as part of a new way of working.

There are lots of non urgent and non life threatening crimes that can be reported online for police reference generation and subsequent action if needed. In Nigeria currently, if you lose your credit card and simply want to report it for insurance purpose, you have to physically visit a police station.

This is not efficient or user friendly. This should also encourage the police to establish multiple access channels for the people to contact it.

From, text, web, telephone, email to face to face contact, the public should be given more ways of making contact. This will encourage better crime reporting, especially by lots of people who distrust the police.

RECOMMENDATION 31:

As part of a new retention policy, all serious professional misconduct by serving officers should automatically trigger open public hearing or open report of internal investigatory findings. This will reassure the distrusting public of the seriousness of change in the police. It will also demonstrate how seriously the police authorities take such matters.

So a new policy of *presumption of openness* should be made statutory to the police in a new Police Act.

- What constitute 'Serious professional misconduct' should be agreed by the Senate after wide consultation with all stakeholders.

RECOMMENDATION 32:

Police officers found guilty of serious professional misconduct should not only be dismissed but prosecuted as a minimum wherever possible. They should also be demoted by one rank for pension purposes.

This will serve as deterrent since a professional misconduct verdict will have life long effect of all officers. Currently an officer dismissed for stealing is merely sent away to enjoy his loot. This is not a deterrent.

OTHER GOOD GOVERNANCE RECOMMENDATIONS

RECOMMENDATION 33:
An Inspectorate of Police should be established with powers to visit, examine, assess and report on performance of police formations nationwide.

This Inspectorate should be required to produce Biannual reports on his/her assessment of the performance and compliance of the police with their constitutional mandate with recommendations as applicable. This Inspectorate should be established outside the police setup and should report to the President directly.

The new Inspectorate will not only be able to inspect police activities and report on it, but will also provide independent support to the police against potentially baseless accusations or unfounded criticism.

The reports of the Inspectorate should as a matter of norm be published for all to read.

- The Police Inspectorate (PI) should also be given power and resources to inspect all the state commands of the police and create a ratings system for each command.

- There should be statutory duty on the IGP and all police commands to cooperate with the Inspectorate. Full access to all reports, intelligence and records should be statutorily granted.

- An example is an Outstanding, Good, Requires Improvement and Poor rating standards. The rating system should ensure certain rating levels will automatically trigger certain intervention or benefits as applicable.

- Poorly rated state commands should elicit immediate direct intervention and the Commissioner in charge should be retired by law.

- Some of the money saved from abolishing the current Ministry of Police Affairs and Police Service Commission can be used to establish this Inspectorate.

RECOMMENDATION 34:

Any police officers involved in shooting of a member of the public should be immediately put on desk duty until a determination of whether the shooting is a "Good" or "Bad" shooting.

- Good shooting should require legitimate self defence or protection of another to be present.

- Bad shooting will be careless, negligent or misconduct shooting.

- A statutory determination of the classification of the shooting must be made within 7days (as an example).

- Bad shootings can then be investigated more thoroughly after this initial determination. This investigation can be done internally by the police, but the proposed Inspectorate will have full access to examine these and report on them.

RECOMMENDATION 35:

To improve public confidence in the police, all police spokespersons must be put under a new statutory duty not to mislead the public. Misleading the people or the media should become gross misconduct and sacking offence.

People must be able to trust statements made by the police. This will help increase confidence in the police and earn them much needed public goodwill and support.

RECOMMENDATION 36:

There should be new training on evidence gathering and use of evidence contextually rolled out to all serving officers. This will include the use of crime scene technologies and other modern evidence techniques.

The research finds a widespread use of summary punishment and torture by the police to elicit confession and sometimes just for punishment of suspects. Eighty percent of interviewed officers agreed that they are ill equipped in the intricacies of evidence gathering.

This habit of physically assaulting suspects has led to lazy policing techniques where there is an over-reliance on induced confessions. Many officers interviewed do not know any other way to gather evidence outside of beating a confession out of the suspect. This training and equipment as applicable in more evidence gathering techniques will create the needed alternative to induced confessions and strengthen good governance.

RECOMMENDATION 37:

A *"Federal Police, Local Policy"* system should be developed. Nigeria operates a centralised national police with states not having power to establish a state police. This research supports the continuation of a federal police structure as mandate by the Constitution[168].

But the priorities of the police in each state and divisions should reflect local needs and preference rather than a nationally imposed operational priorities.

This will mean Nigeria will continue to operate a national police but with locally decided priorities. This will create more local accountability for the police, thus improving links with the communities. This will also begin

---

[168] Section 214 (1) of 1999 Constitution of Nigeria as amended

to sow the seed of policing by consent in the minds of serving officers.

If the police prioritise the most important issues to local communities, they will in turn get better cooperation from those communities. The principle of consent in policing is essential to secure public buy-in into police activities.

RECOMMENDATION 38:

Police should be brought under more local democratic accountability, even with a federal police command structure. A new State Advisory Boards (SABs) should be stablished by statute for each state command of the police.

- The SAB should include all key stakeholders in the state. This is not a security panel meeting the state Governors have with security chiefs in the state. The SAB will enable each local areas bring to the table their top local challenges for the State Police Commissioner to review, respond and action. SABs should consist of the following representatives:

- o State government

- o Local government

- o Wider criminal Justice community (Prison, Prosecution authorities etc)

- o Civic Society

- o Relevant NGOs (for example the CLEEN Foundation or Amnesty International)

- o Ordinary citizens

- o Representatives of Organised Religious Associations, etc

Police should build and strengthen key relationships at the local and state levels in order to develop support, consent and cooperation from the communities to fight crime and fulfil its constitutional mandate. Membership of the SAB will be unpaid and on voluntary basis.

RECOMMENDATION 39:

As many of the recommendation in this book require both Constitutional and Other Statutes changes, It is recommended that name of the police be change from the Nigeria Police Force to *The Nigerian Police Service.*

This word 'Force' reinforces the militarised thrust and disposition of the police and make it look like an arm of the Military rather than a service to the community. This change will also have a psychological impact on serving officers that they are not a force unit but service providers to the public.

RECOMMENDATION 40:

It is recommended that the National Assembly produce a new expanded police Act that will be all encompassing and contain all the body of laws, rules, procedures and operational standards for the police in Nigeria. As noted in Chapter 6, there are several instruments that gives the police their powers from the Constitution to the Police Act to Force Manuals and so on.

This has created a confused body of legal instruments. The recommended consolidation will mean that aside from the Constitution, only this new Police Act will be used as the legal bible for the police. This will get rid of colonial legal instruments and multiple and sometime contradictory power tools.

RECOMMENDATION 41:

The police need more sources of funding in addition to their statutory grants from the government. It is recommended that a state level Strategic Partnership Board (SPB) be established in every state.

The SPB will bring together key stakeholders in the private sector and community in the state to assist the police in raising funds and sponsorships as needed.

The state commands will have a list of priority projects and initiatives that need funding. The SPB will use its influence to get private sector involvement in support of the police in each state. Membership of the SPB should include:

- Police representatives
- Representatives of the organised private sector in the state, (for instance, the Chambers of Commerce etc.)
- Representative of Traditional institutions (such as Kings and chiefs)
- Representatives from leading corporations within the state
- Representatives of the Academia

RECOMMENDATION 42:

The IGP should be mandated to provide periodical (biannual or quarterly) accounts of his stewardship to the nation. This should include accounting for what has happened to all his previously announced directives.

Ninety percent of people interviewed (both within the police and ordinary citizens) stated that most of the announced directives from the IGP are never implemented and there is no accountability by the IGP for the non compliance to his many directives.

An example cited by many interviewed relates to the use of Checkpoints on major roads by the police.[169] There have been multiple announcements by IGPs that these checkpoints should stop,[170] but they still persists[171] and nothing has been done about it.

This complete disregard for a public directive[172] of the IGP by the various command levels can further weaken the confidence of the public in the police institution. This must change.

---

[169] < http://www.nigerianelitesforum.com/ng/security-military-and-para-military-forces/3766-police-checkpoints-banned-nationwide.html> accessed on 20 February 2016

[170] < http://www.pmnewsnigeria.com/2010/08/30/police-checkpoints-banned/> accessed on 18 February 2016

[171] < http://www.premiumtimesng.com/news/3807-police-officers-disregard-ig_s-order-police-checkpoints-everywhe.html> accessed on 20 February 2016

[172] < http://nationalmirroronline.net/new/illegal-police-checkpoints-still-on-highways-survey/> accessed on 20 February 2016

RECOMMENDATION 43:

To address some of the legitimate concerns of the VIPs and elite about crime and personal protection, especially given the widespread use of kidnapping as ways of extorting money by criminals, an elite rank of private security firms (with powers to carry arms) should be established in the country.

Nigeria has a well establish private security industry albeit unarmed at the moment. This elite group of private security firms should be well regulated and trained. This will be commercial operations between the firms and its customers, thus freeing up the official police personnel to conduct frontline policing.

And as stated earlier in this chapter, this could release over 100,000 police personnel for frontline work.

A regulator paid for by the industry should be setup to enforce standards and ensure public policy interests are protected.

HOW TO MAKE THESE RECOMMENDATIONS WORK?

How can these recommendations be put to work? A number of these recommendations clearly have cost implications for the government. There is need for a root and branch review of the funding of the police in Nigeria. The government need to find the additional funding needed to support good governance in the police. Some of these recommendations can pay for themselves.

For instance, with Nigeria allegedly losing almost $1.7 billion[173], (about N272 billion) per month to oil theft, vandalism and bunkering, More effective and better equipped police force will reduce this loss significantly, thus increasing the revenue of government (regardless of the actual figure of such loss in the future). If the police were able to reduce

---

[173] Bamidele Olowosagba, 'SHOCKER: Nigeria Ranks Highest In Crude Oil Theft' (Naij.com - Nigeria news., 2014) <https://www.naij.com/69464.html> accessed 11 February 2016.

these crimes by just 50 per cent, that is an extra N136Billion additional monthly income for the government yearly.

Paying for these recommendations will be possible from such significant additional government revenue. Of course with the price of oil very volatile at the moment, the exact amount of savings will vary.

The Strategic partnerships recommended in the state commands, will also raise more funds and sponsorship for the police in the states across the country. A more pro-active high level policing culture and capability will also cut down on crime.

This will reduce the cost to the courts and prison service as well as to the wider criminal justice system. Reduction in crime will also lead to a happier population who will become more productive and more willing to support the government and the police.

It is hoped that these recommendations if implemented will have a dramatic impact on the Resources available, Recruitment and Training of police officers in the country. Developing good governance in any organisation will require elements of change management.

From stakeholder's engagement, change impact analysis, role impact analysis, training needs analysis to change readiness activities and ultimately benefits realisation of the change initiative.

With collective good will and support for the Nigerian police, change is possible and achievable.

FINALLY

It is recommended that the President set up an independent commission with the task of working on the implementation of these and any other recommendations that may exist on supporting good governance in Nigerian police force. This commission will develop implementation timelines and be able to liaise with the Senate to recommend needed legislative changes and consolidation as recommended.

It is recommended that this commission report not only to the President, but should publish quarterly reports to the public as well as open press conferences. Nigerians need to be carried along and reassured in its work.

Appendix 1

Financial Impact Classification
Table of All Recommendations

Those WITH Additional financial implication	Those WITHOUT additional Financial implication	Those that can potentially SAVE MONEY
1, 2, 4, 6, 10, 11, 12, 13, 14, 19, 21, 26, 28, 30, 33, 36	3, 5, 7, 8, 9, 18, 22, 23, 24, 25, 27, 29, 31, 32, 34, 35, 37, 38, 39, 40, 42, 43	15, 16, 17, 20, 41

As the above table shows, majority of the recommendations in this book can be implemented Without additional financial implication and quite a few can actually save money. This reality should encourage the government to take on the challenge of implementing them.

Bibliography

1) Adeyemi, A. A. (1993) "Information Management for National Development, Planning and Security" in T. N. Tamuno, I. L. Bashir, E. E. O. Alemika and A. O. Akano eds. *Policing Nigeria : Past, Present and Future* (Lagos : Malthouse Press Limited).

2) Akano, A. O. (1993) "The police, Rule of Law and Human Rights : The police Perspective" in T. N. Tamuno *et al* eds. *Policing Nigeria.*

3) Alemika, E. (1986) "Criminal Justice Principles and Nigerian police Prosecutorial Disposition" *Nigerian Journal of Policy and Strategy* 1(2): 1-17.

4) Alemika E. E. (1988) "Policing and Perceptions of police in Nigeria" *police Studies* 11(4): 161-176.

5) Alemika, E. E. O. (1993a) "Criminology, Criminal Justice and the Philosophy of Policing" in T .N. Tamuno, I. L. Bashir, E .E. O. Alemika and A. O. Akano (eds.)

6) Alemika, E. E. O. (1993b) "Colonialism, State and Policing in Nigeria" *Crime, Law and Social Change* 20: 189-219.

7) Alemika, E. E. O. (1997) "police, Policing and Crime Control in Nigeria" *Nigerian Journal of Policy and Strategy* 12 (1 and 2): 71 - 98.

8) Alemika, E. E. O. and Chukwuma I.C. (2000) - *police-Community Violence in Nigeria* (Centre for Law Enforcement Education, Lagos and the National Human Rights Commission, Abuja, Nigeria)

9) Ali, G. (2008), police and Human Rights Abuse in Nigeria. A seminar paper presented in Department of Sociology, Ahmadu Bello University, Zaria.

10)Claire de Than, etal (2003), International Criminal Law and Human Rights. New York: Thomson, Sweet and Maxwell.

11) Guelke Adrian, 2001. "Crime, Justice and the Legacy of the Past," in *Crime and Policing in Transitional Societies*. (Seminar Report). Johannesburg, RSA: Konrad Adenauer.

12) Comassie, A.I. (1990), Discipline Superior police Officer. A paper presented at the seminar for Area Commanders and Assistant Commissioners of police held at the police Staff College, Jos. March 19 - 23.

13) Comassie,A.I. (1996), The making of the Peoples' police. Lecture delivered at the National Orientation Agency, Abuja.

14) Mohammed, U.J.G.(2011), Human Rights Abuses by police Force in Bosso police Station Minna, Niger State (unpublished Mlc project).

15) Nwankwo,C.D. etal. (1993), Human Rights Practices in the Nigerian police. Constitutional Rights Project, Lagos.

16) Odinkalu, C. (2002) Ed. *Hope Betrayed: A report on Impunity and State-Sponsored*

Violence in Nigeria. Geneva: World Organisation Against Torture and Centre for Law Enforcement Education.

17) Tamuno, T. N (1970) *The Police in Modern Nigeria*: 1861-1965. Ibadan: Ibadan University Press

18) Innes, M., and Thiel, D. (2008) Policing terror In Newburn, T. (ed.) *Handbook of policing*. Cullompton: Willan. pp 553-579.

Coming soon…..

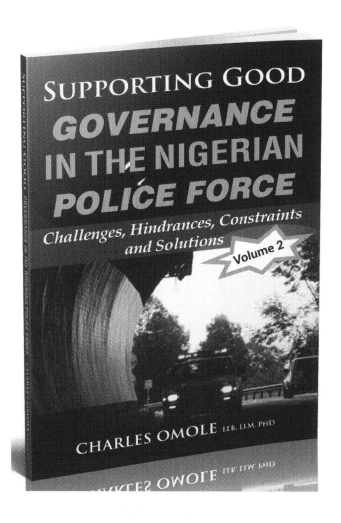

Supporting Good Governance in the Nigerian Police Force.

New Release...

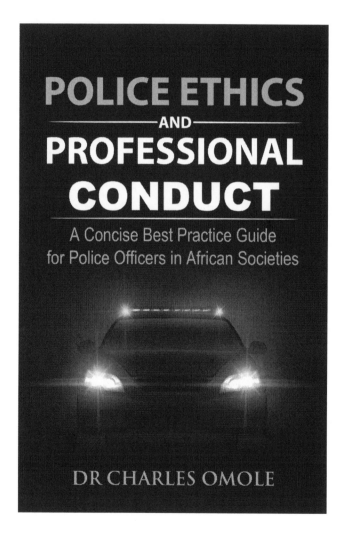

New Release…

Contact Information for Dr. Charles Omole

Charlesomole@Gmail.com

Printed in Poland
by Amazon Fulfillment
Poland Sp. z o.o., Wrocław

62988561R00179